THIS BOOKS BELONGS TO

COLOR TEST PAGE

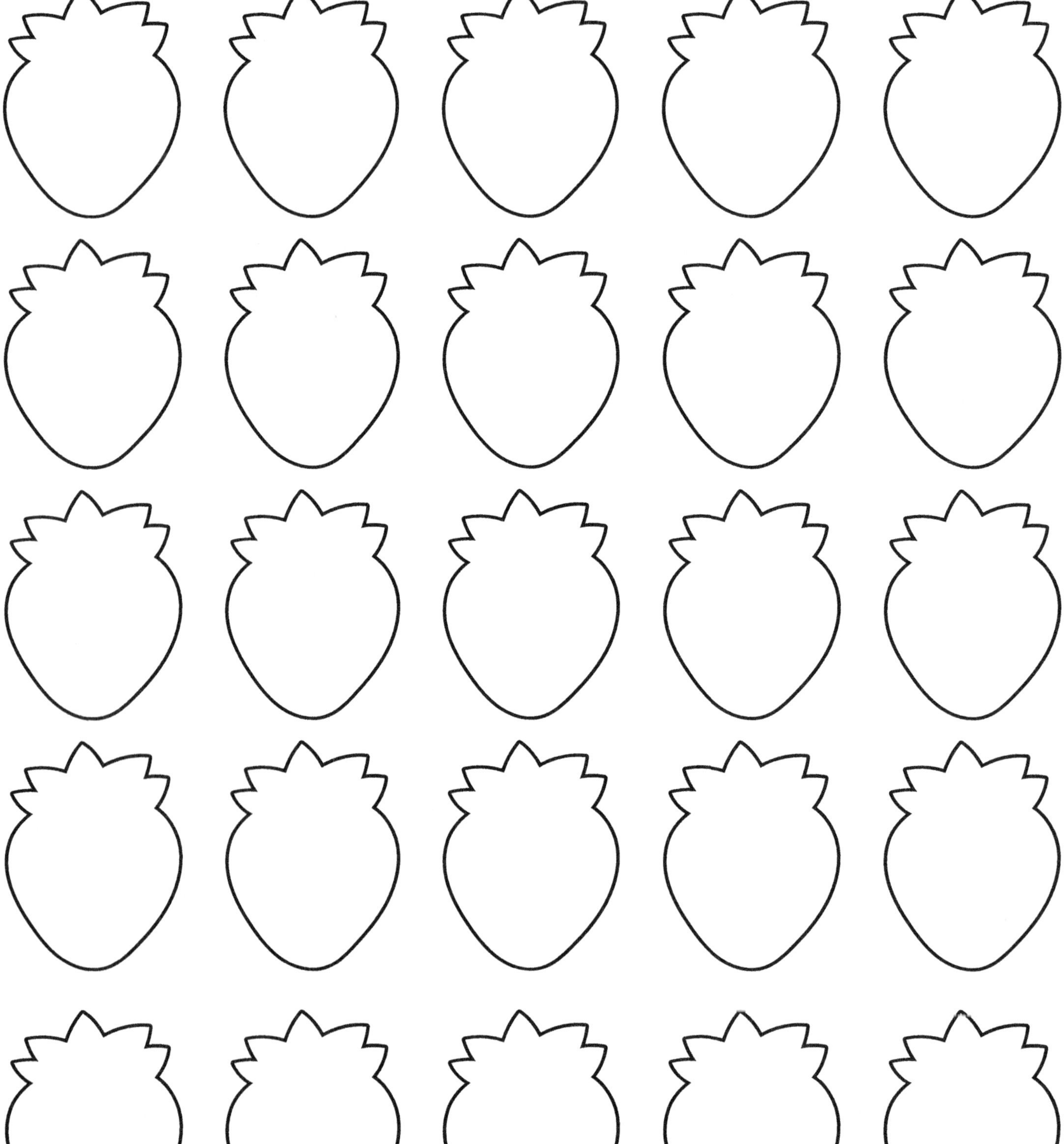

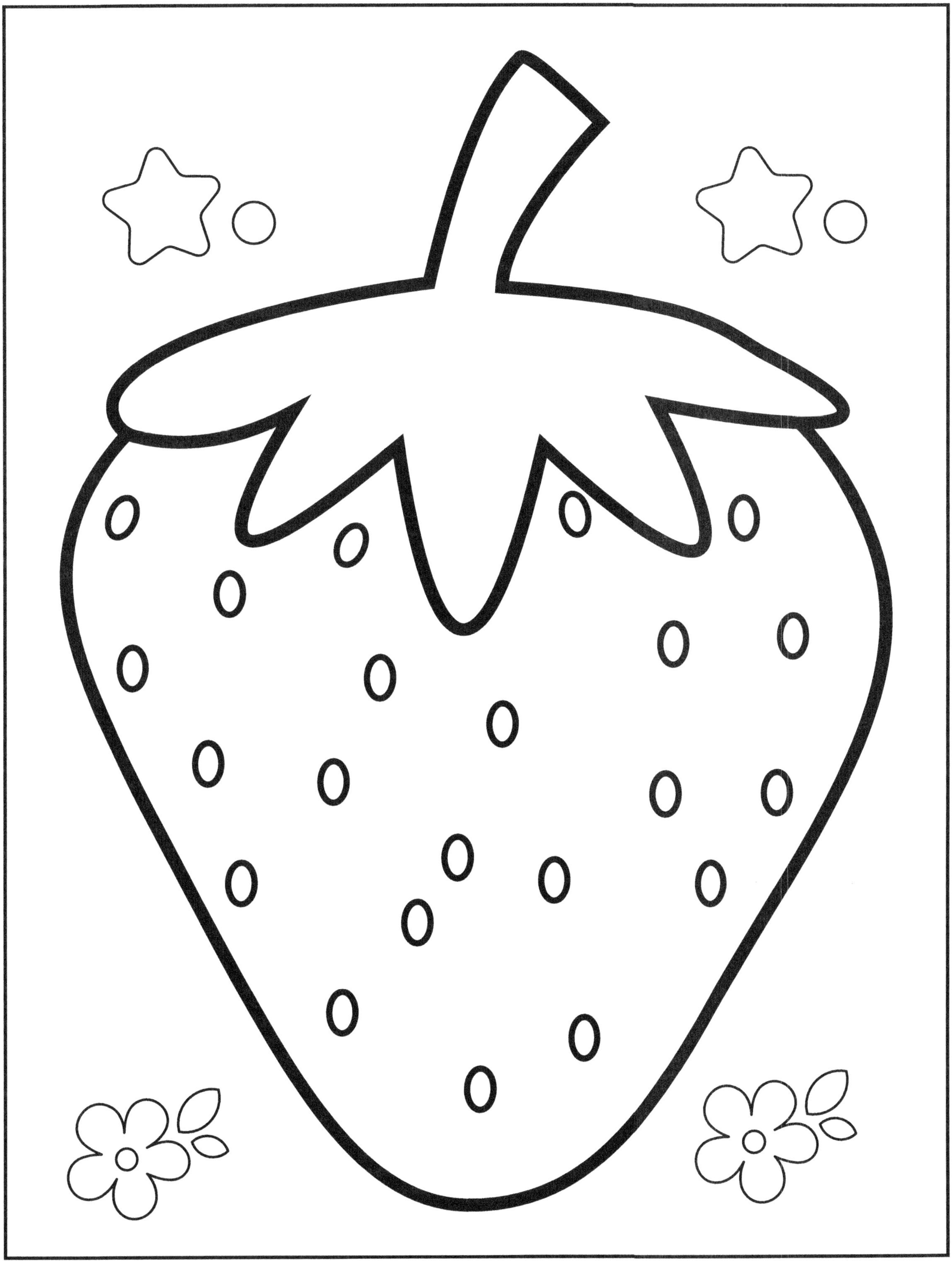

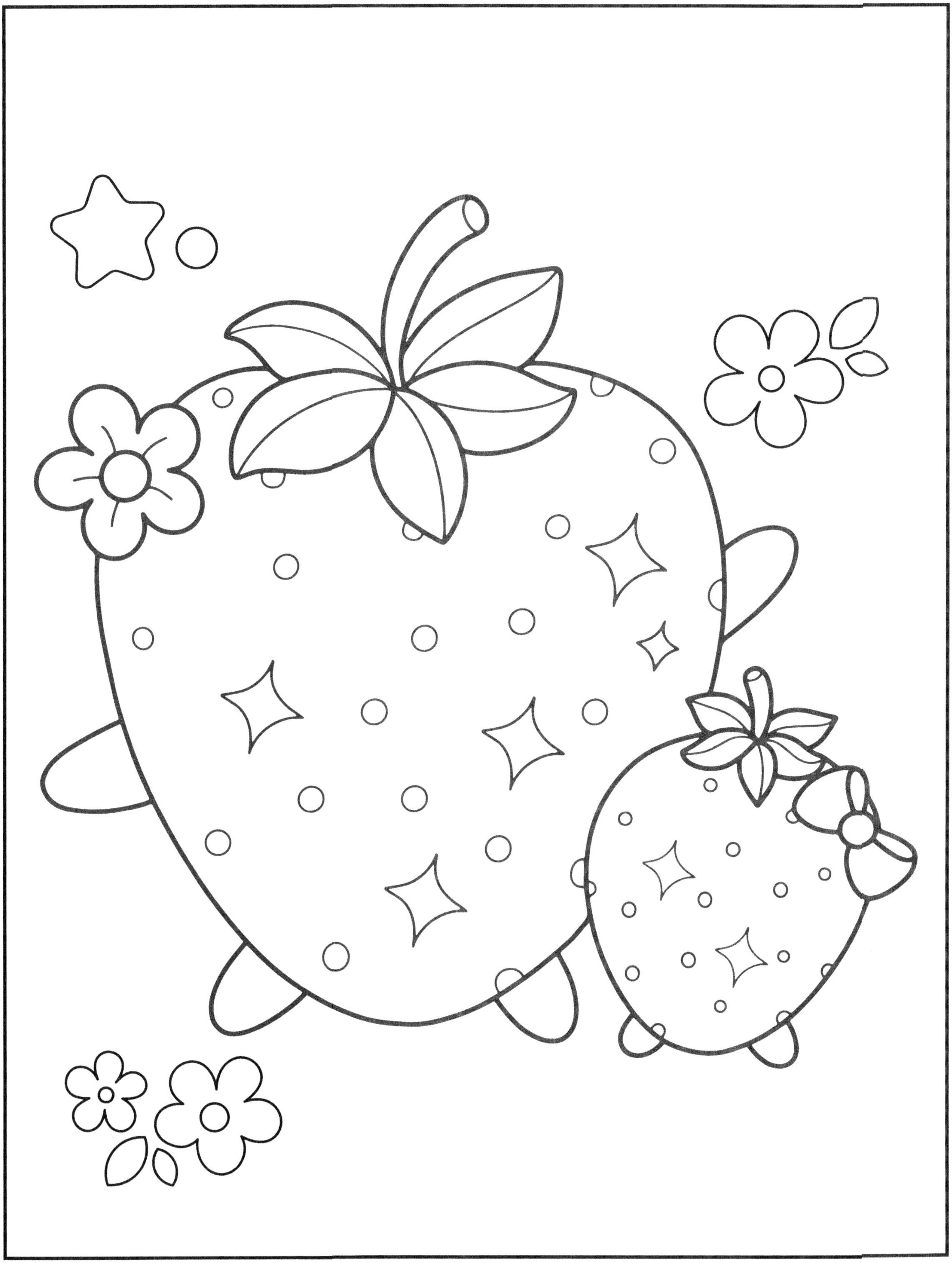

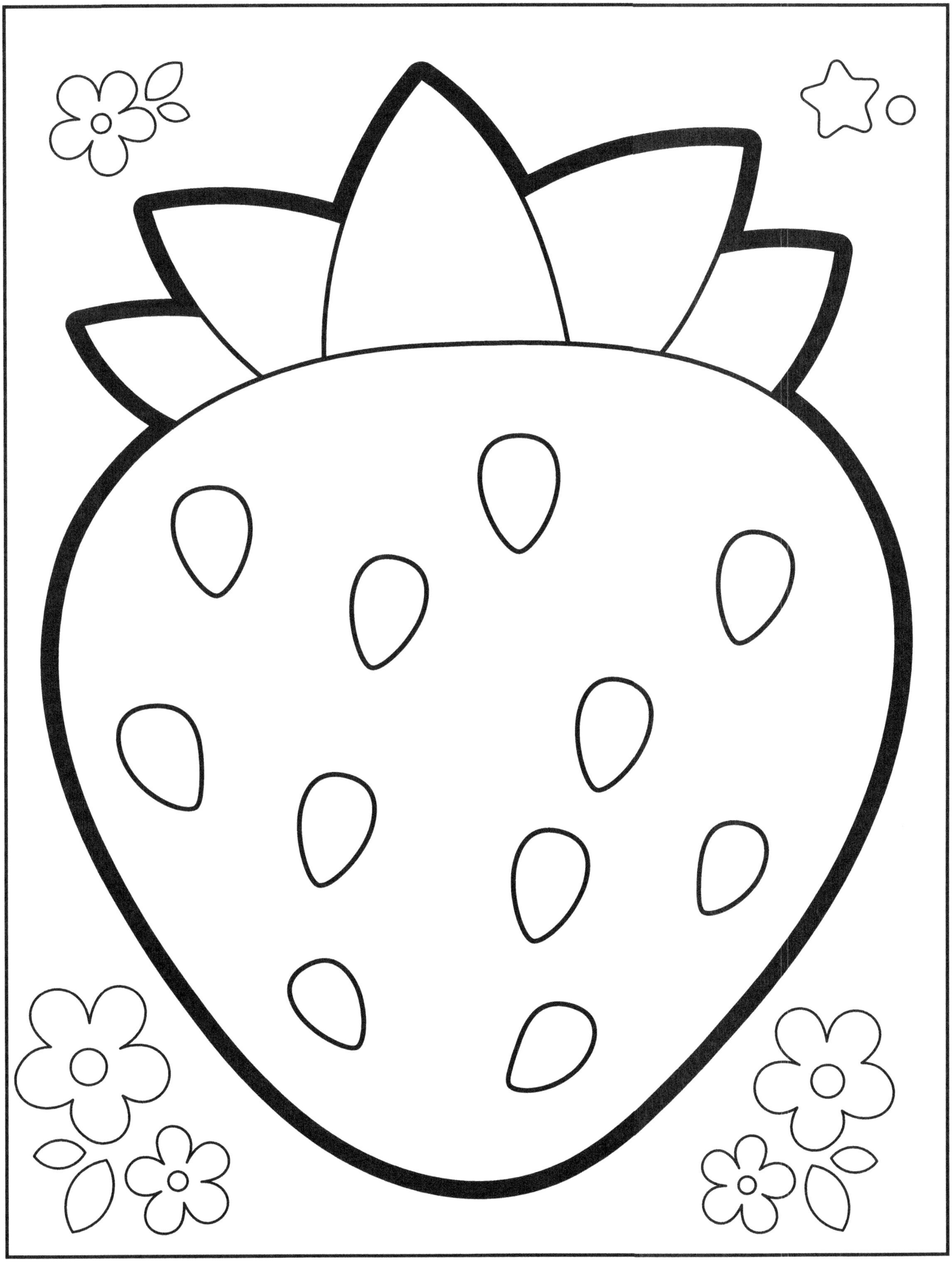

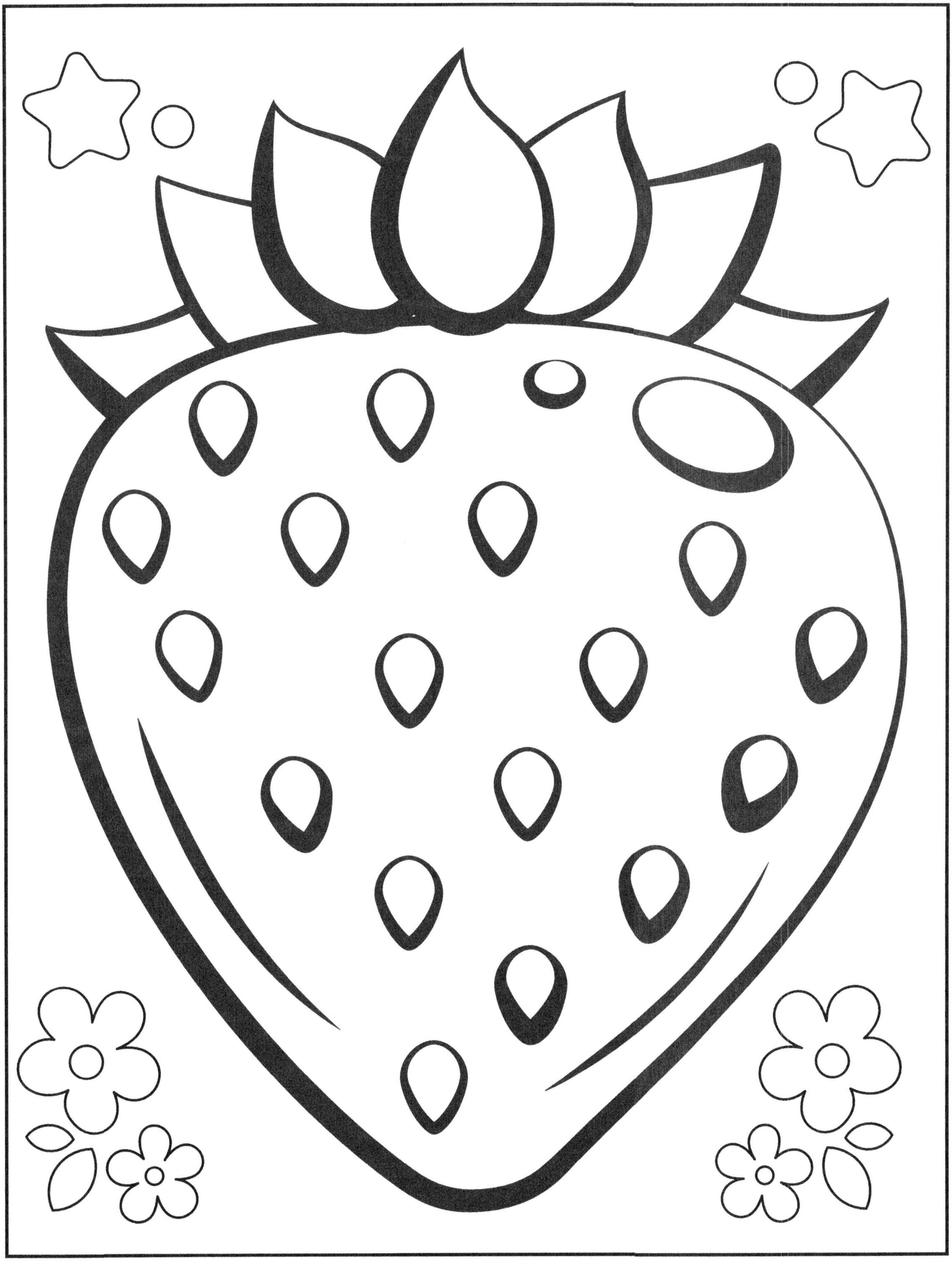

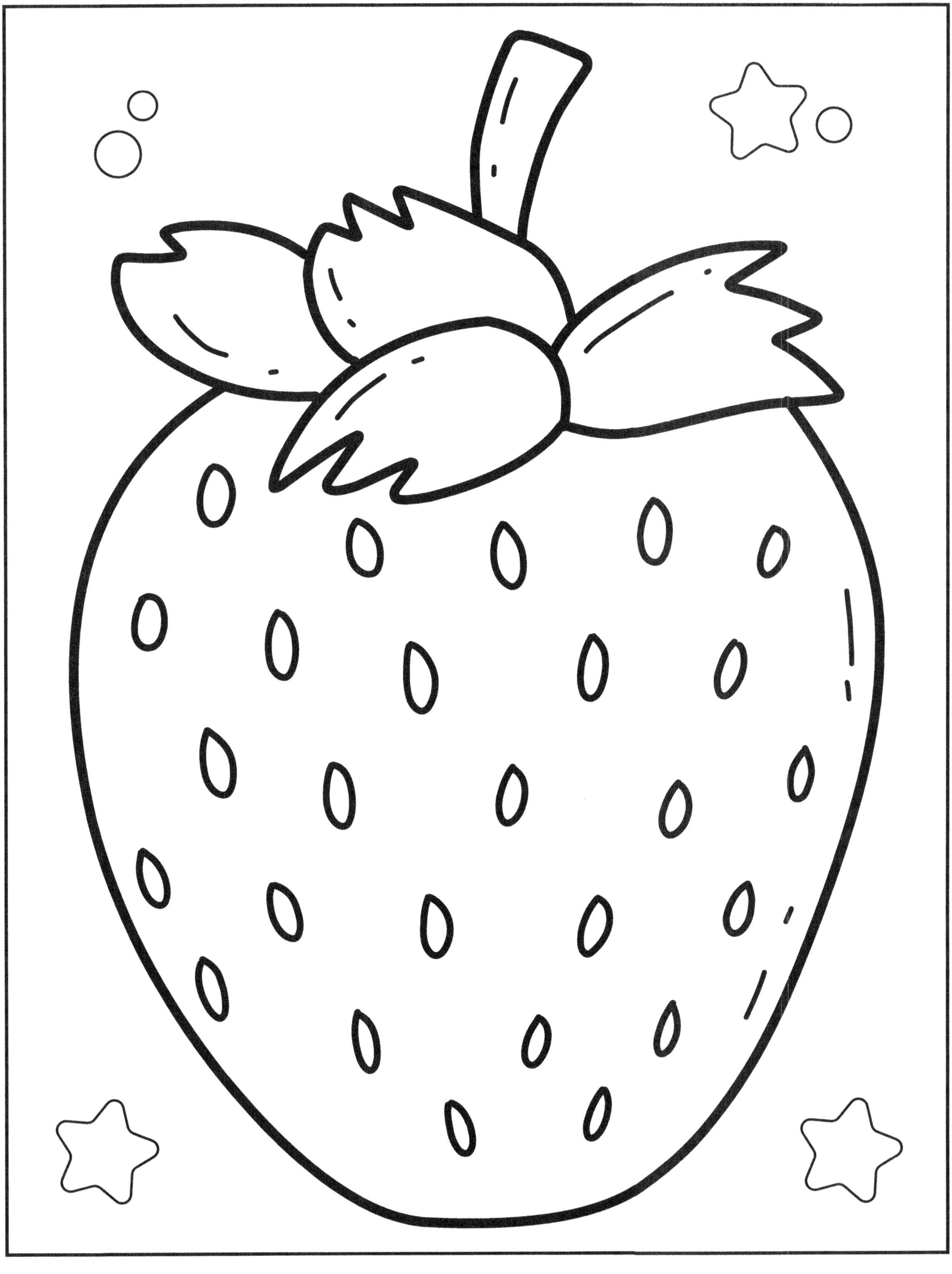

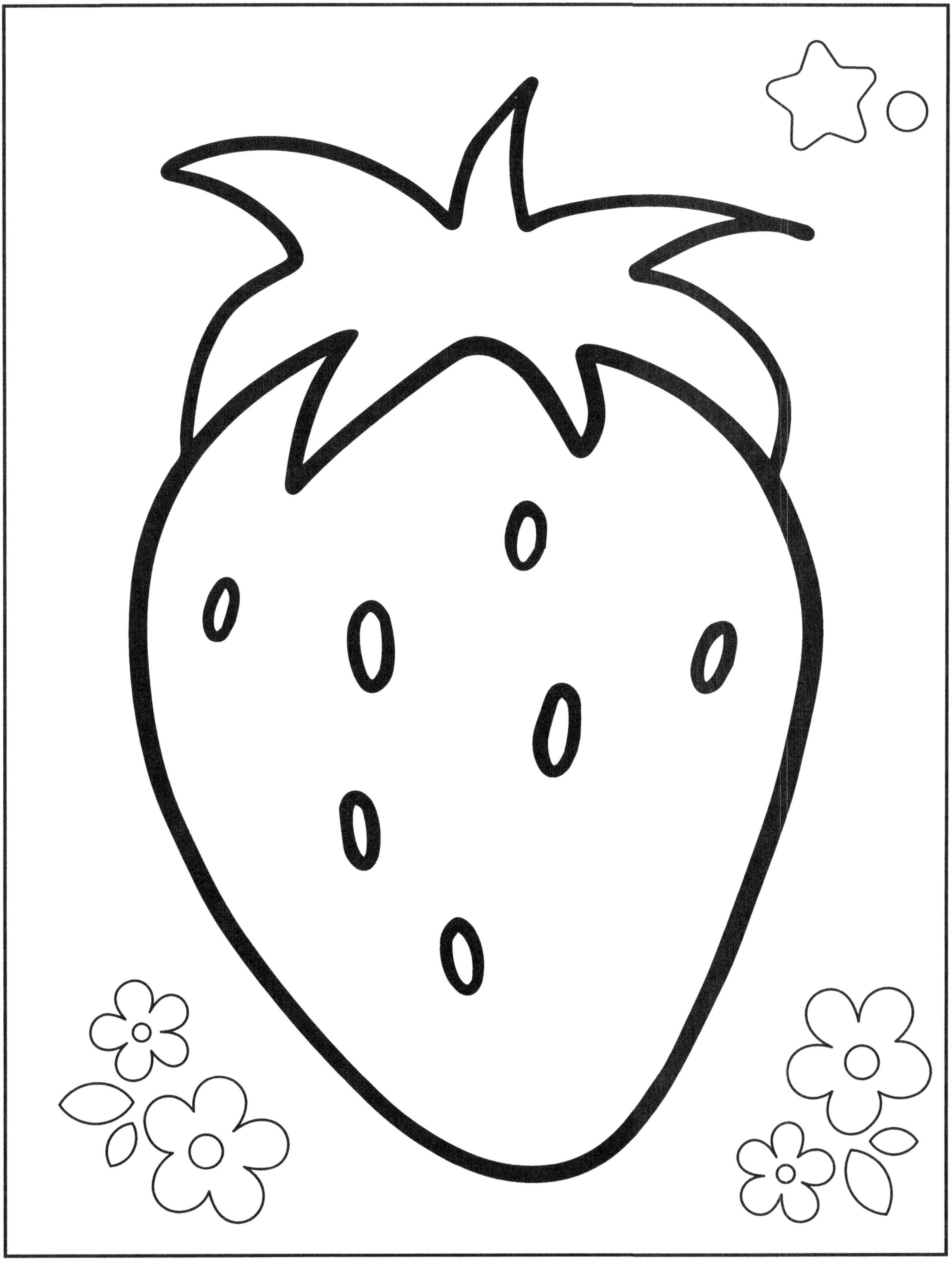

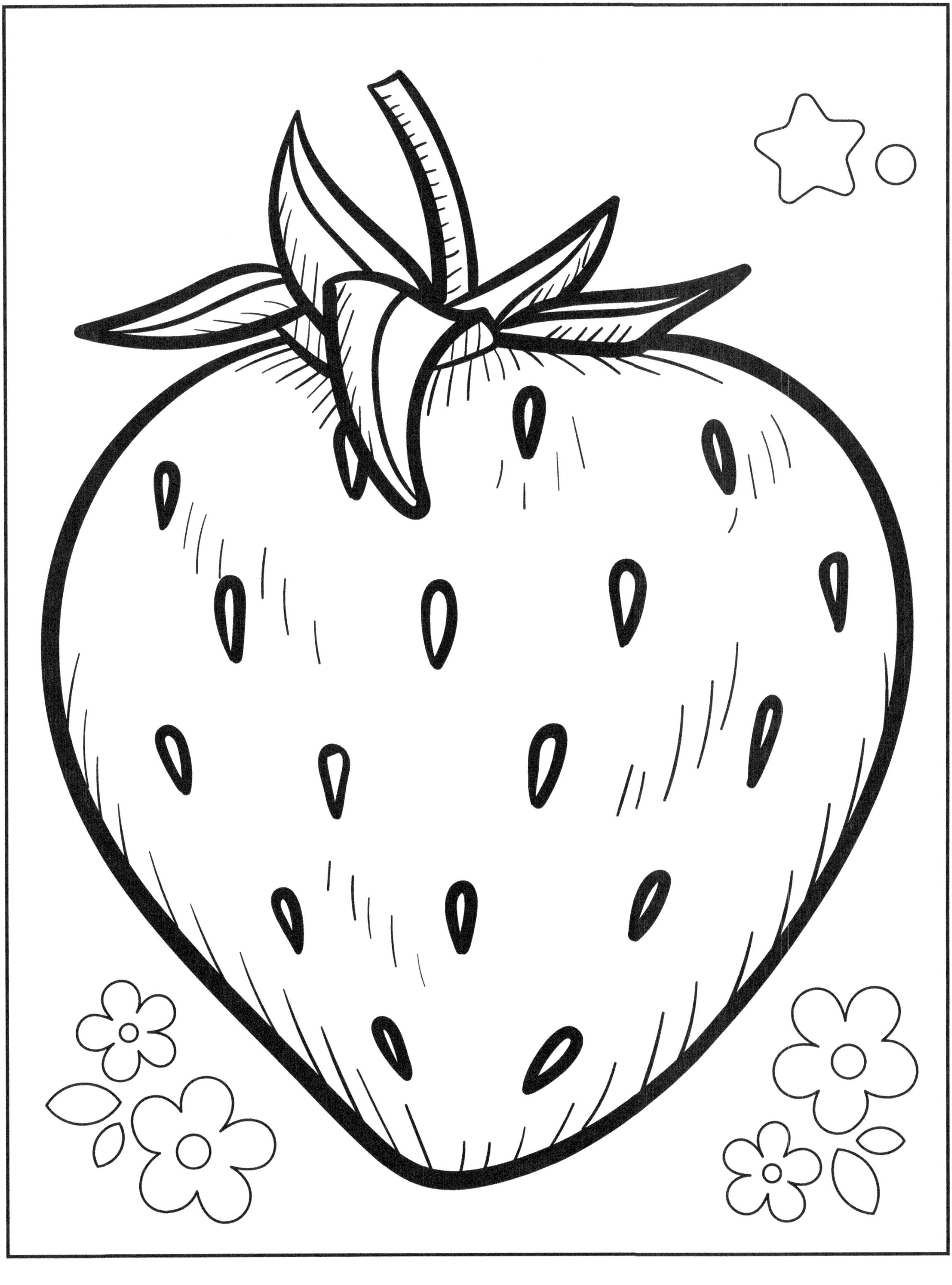

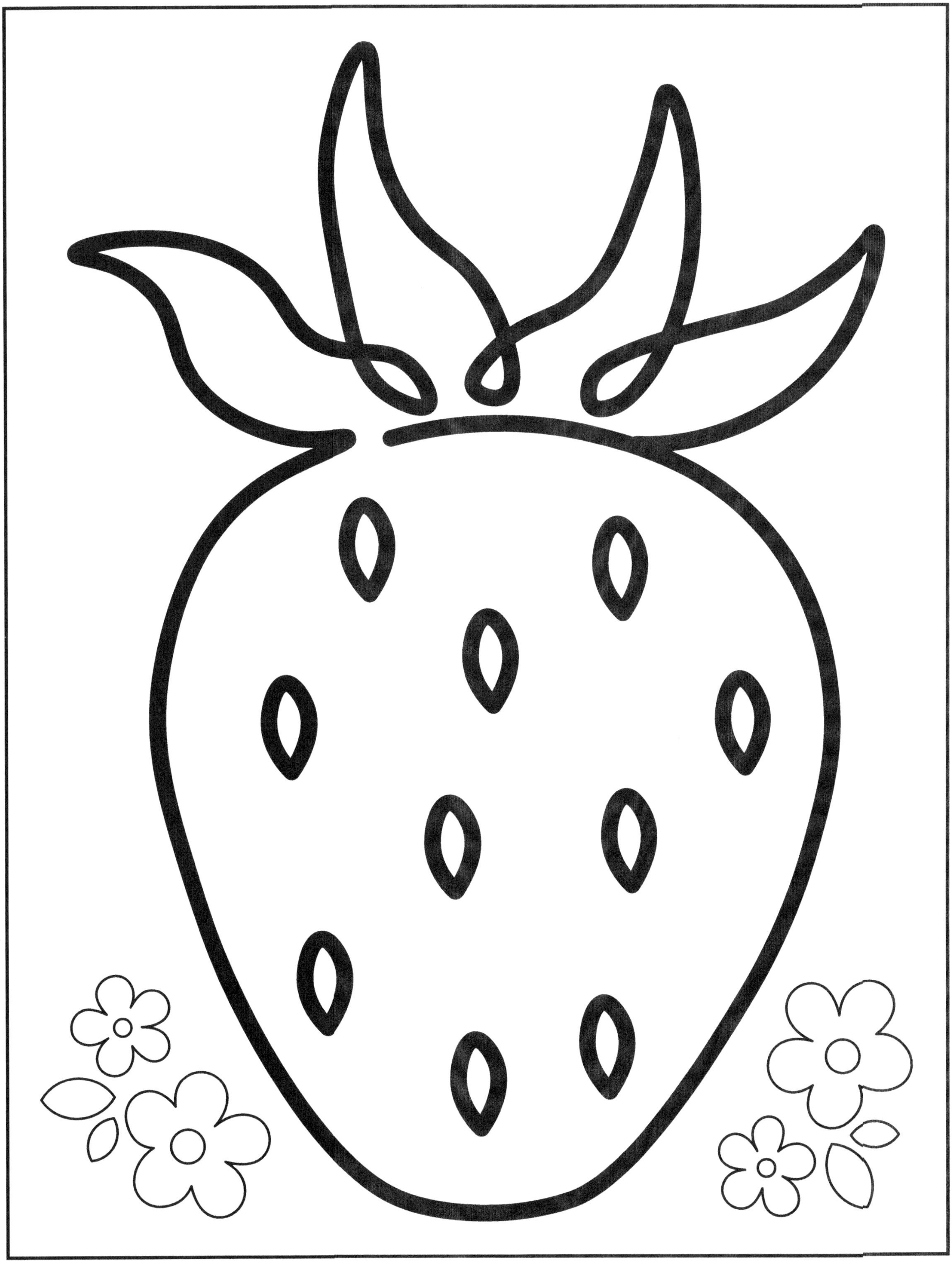

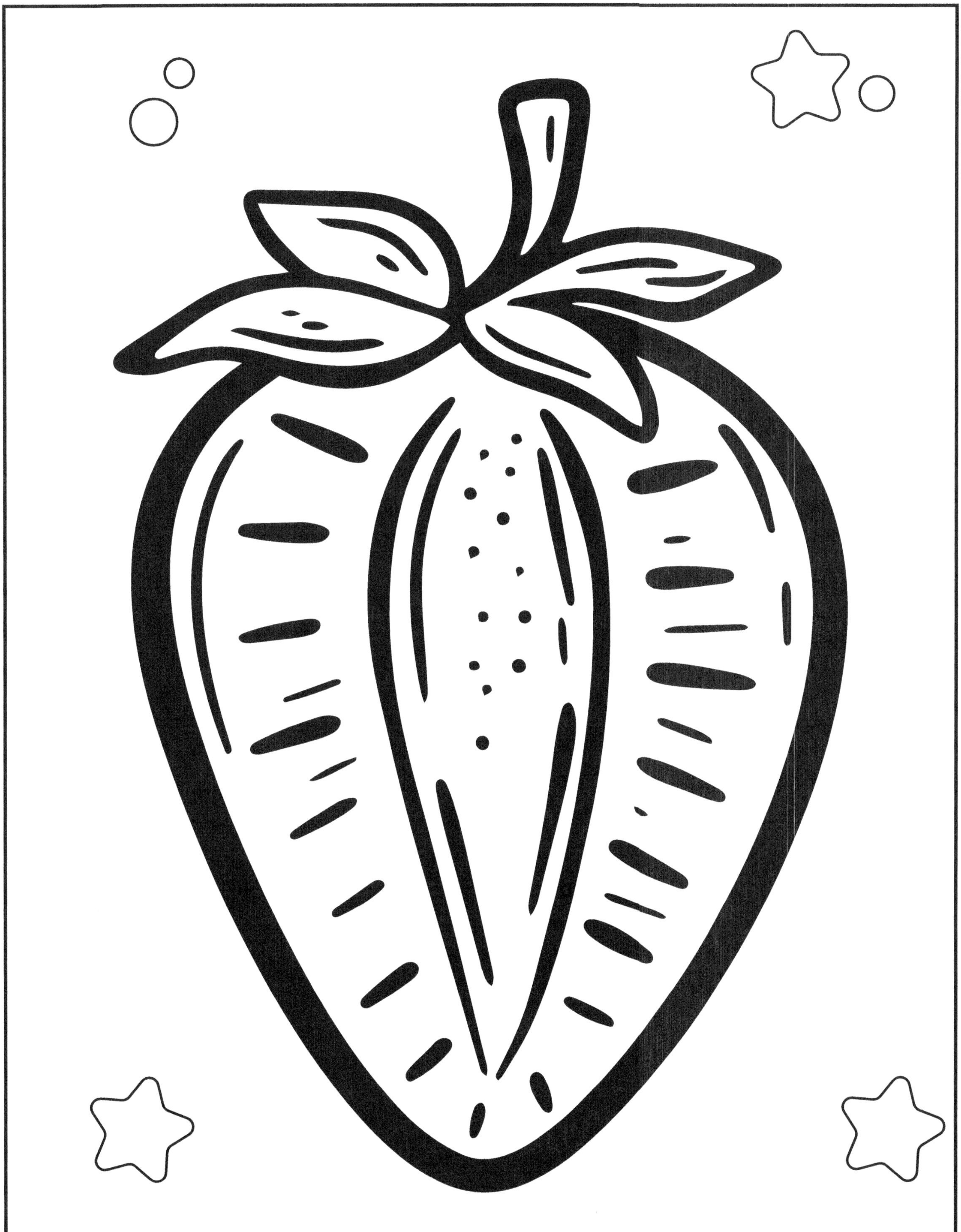

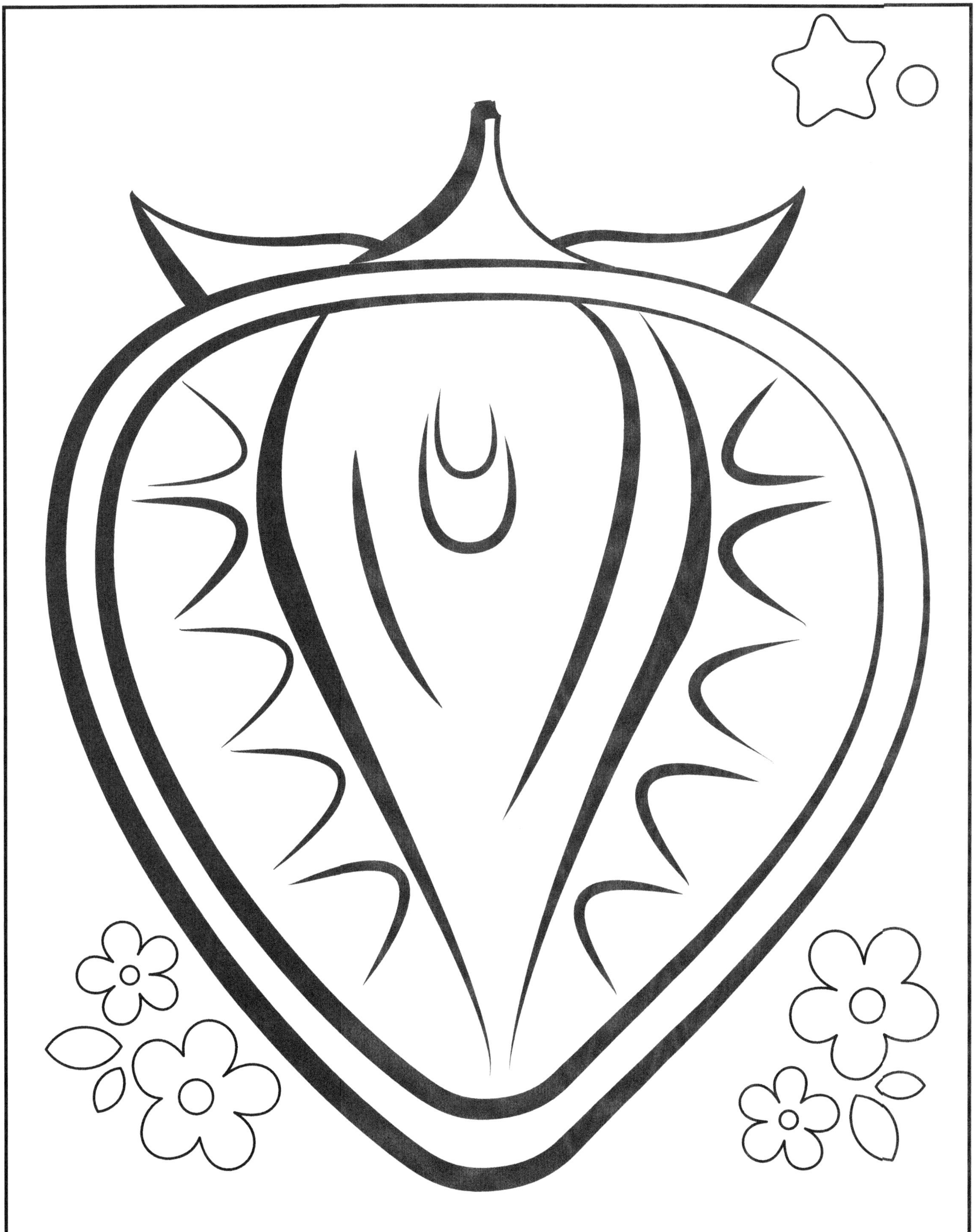

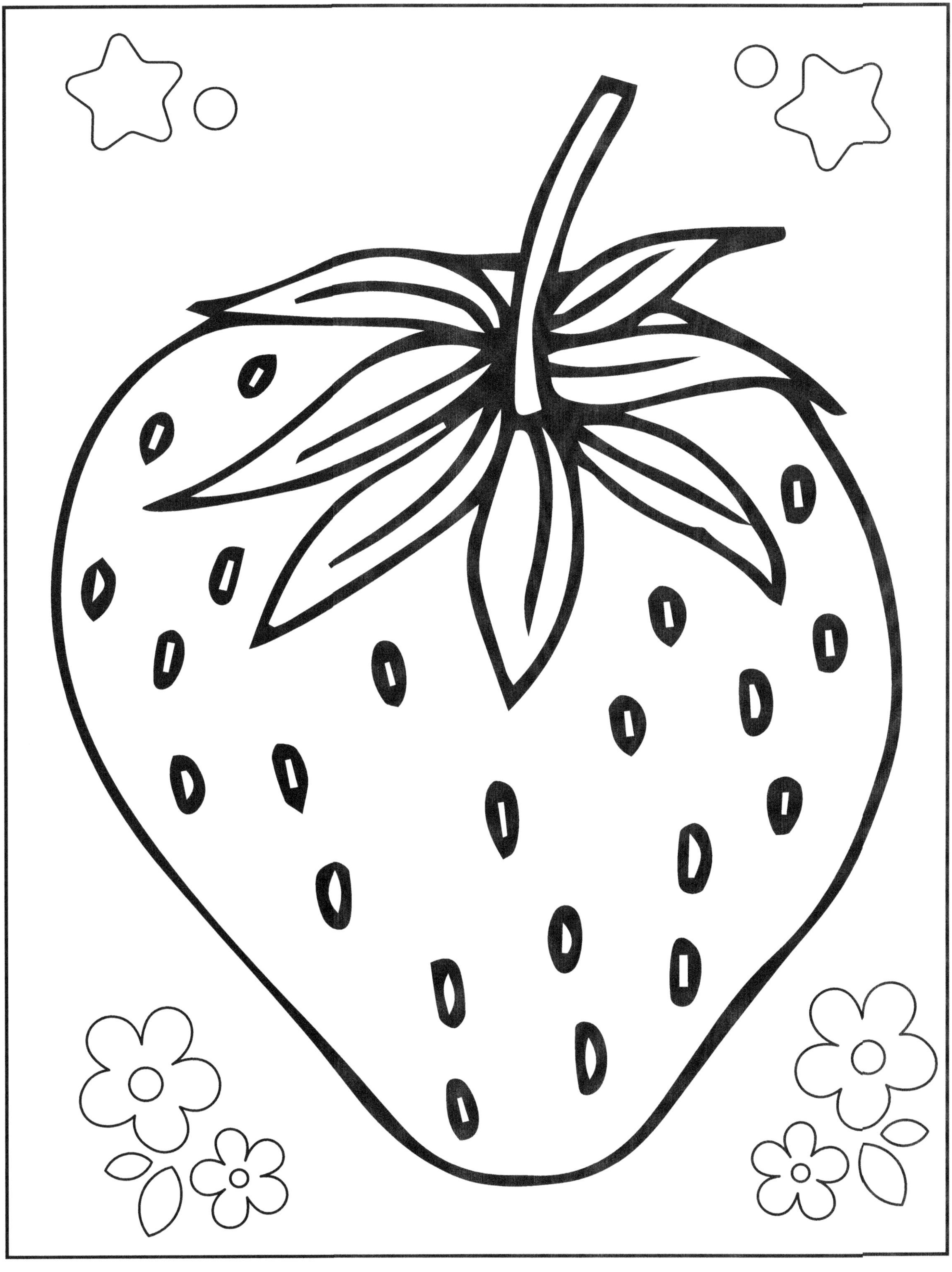

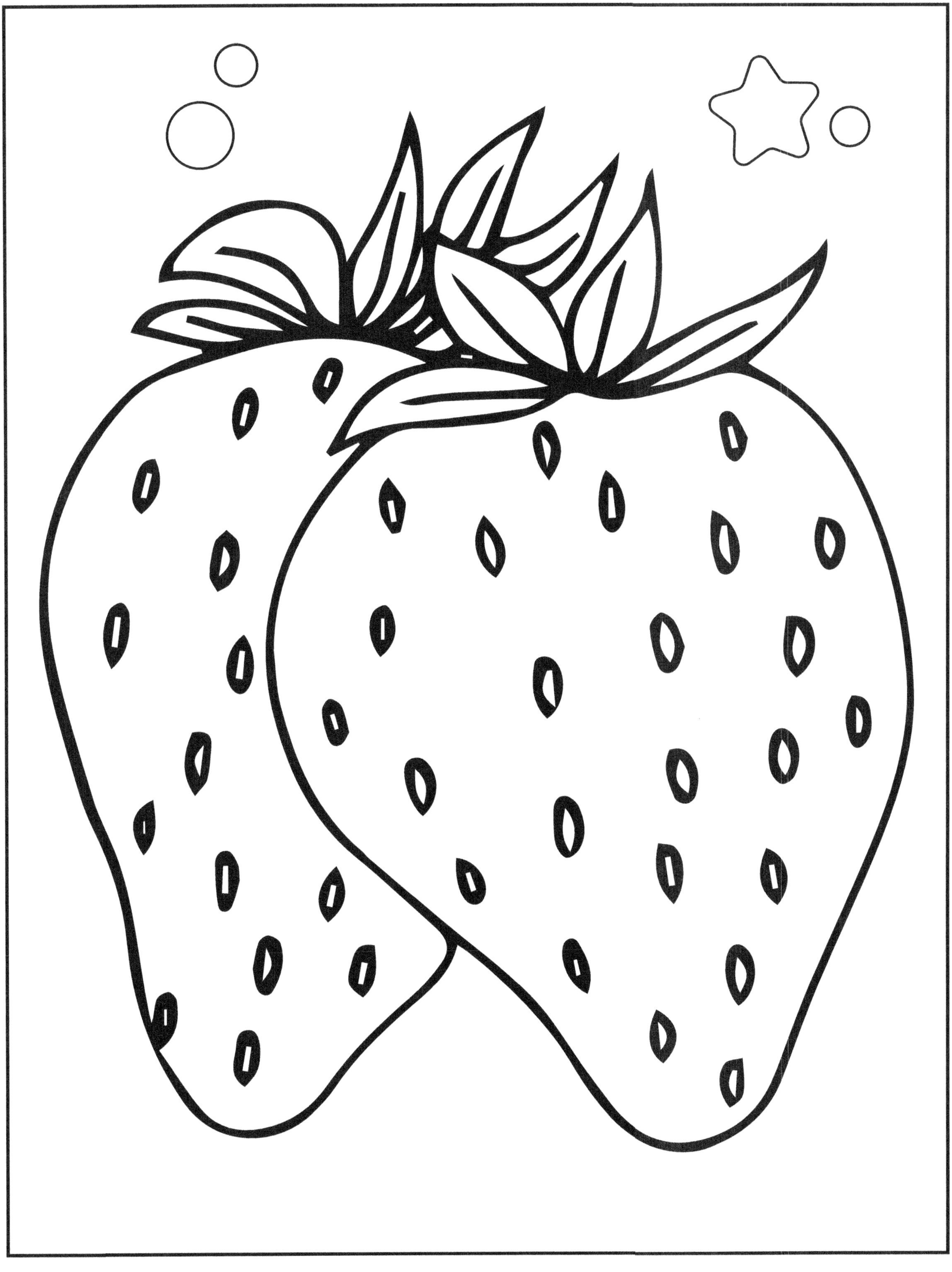

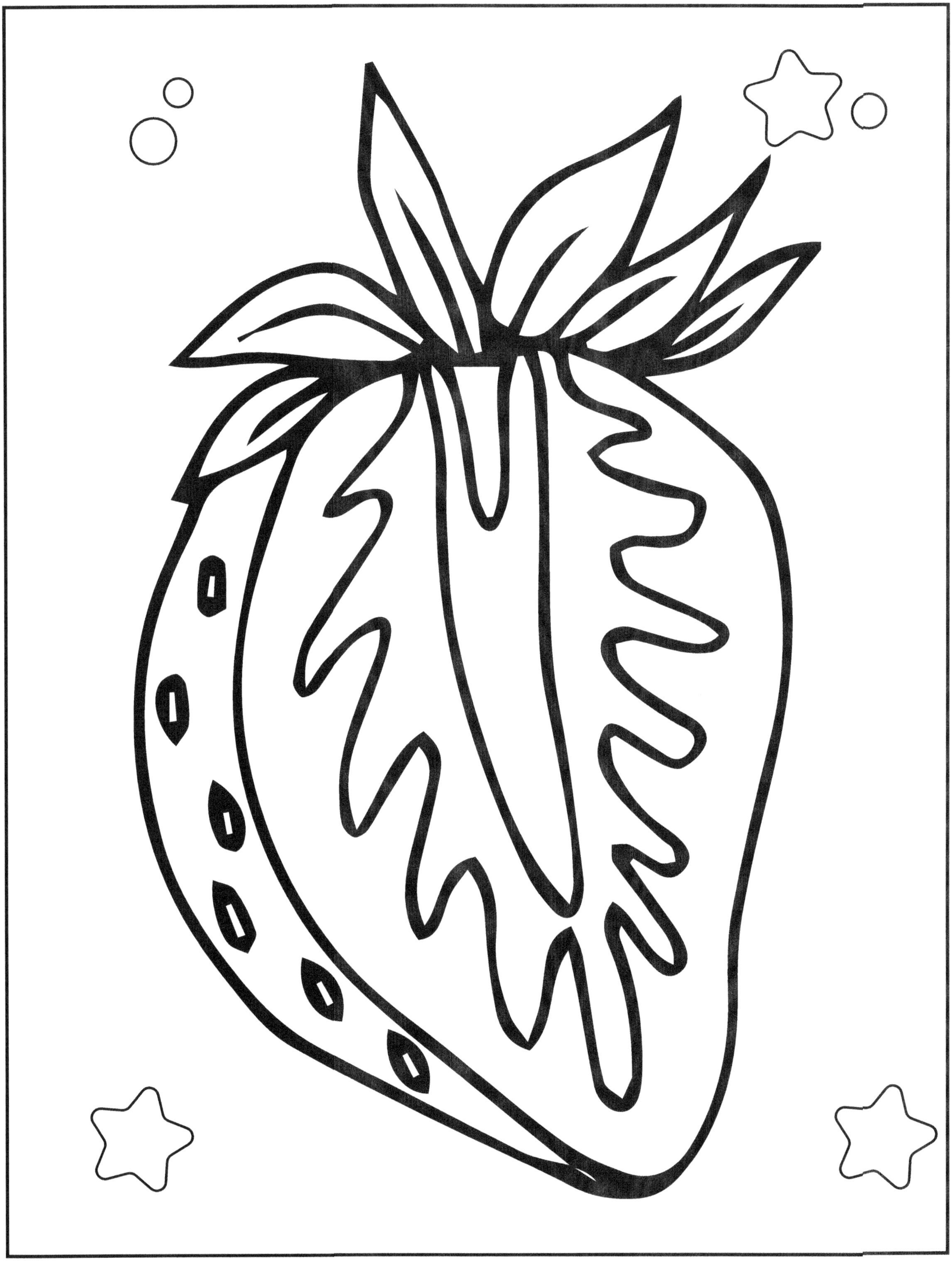

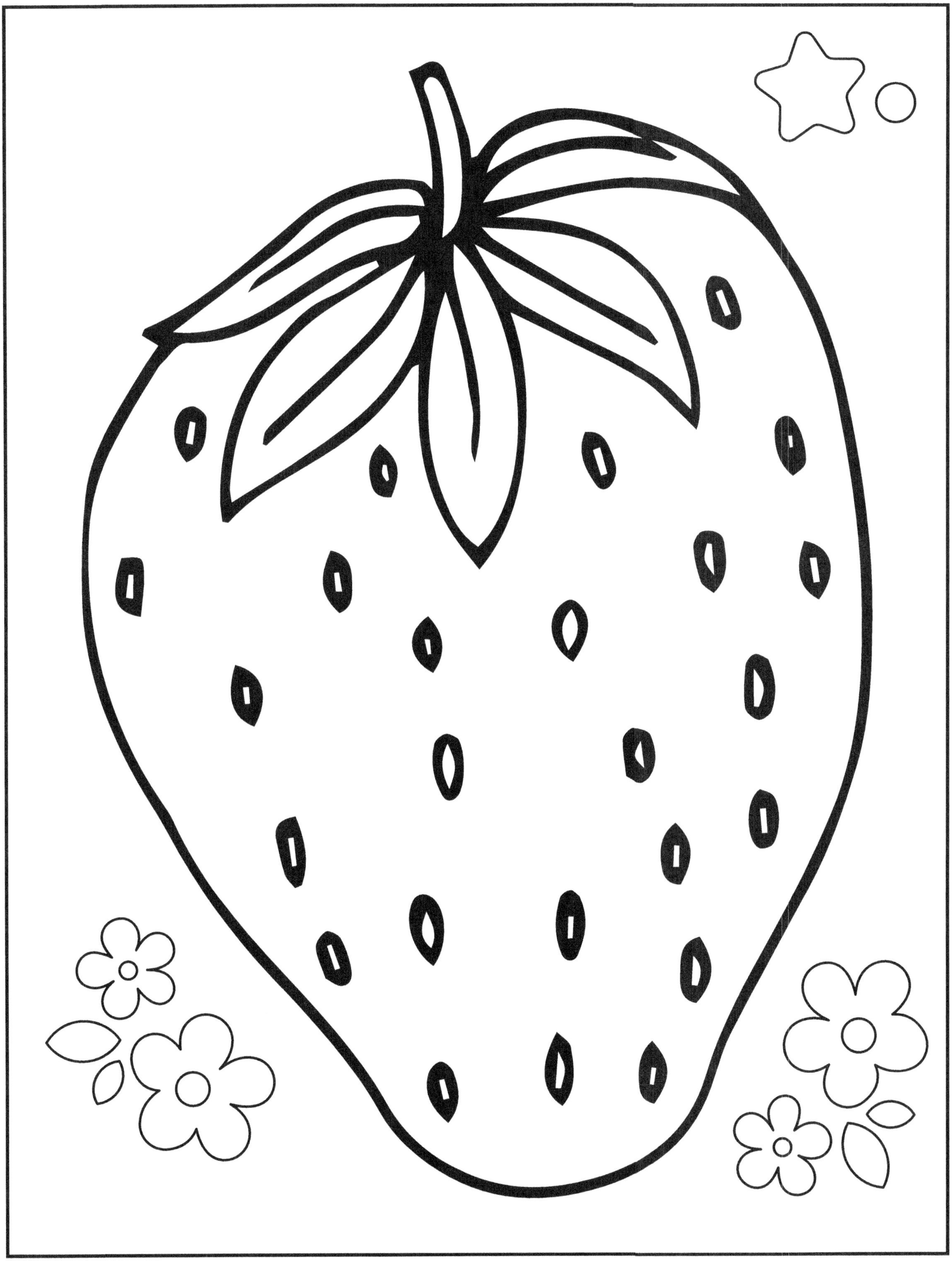

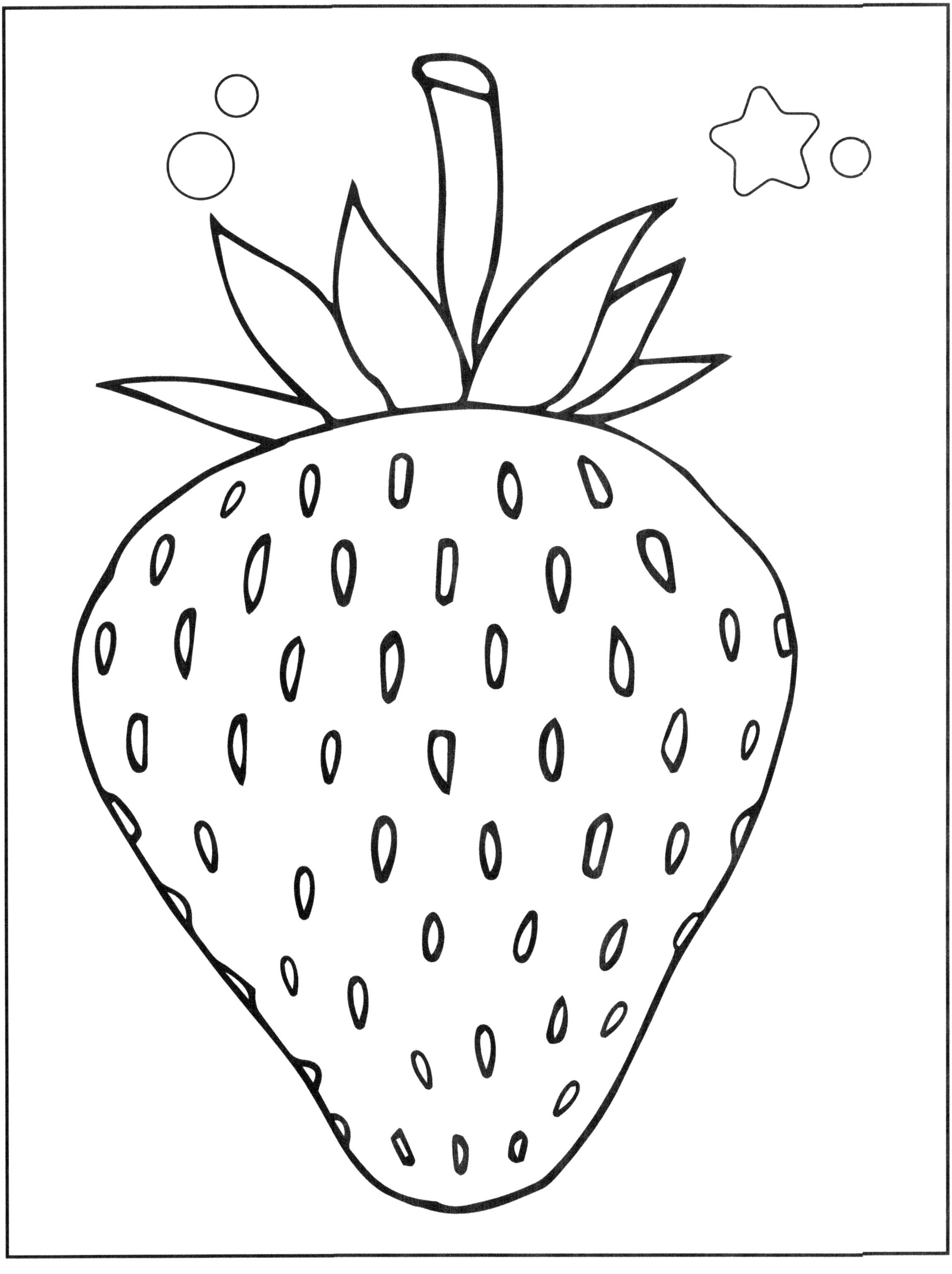

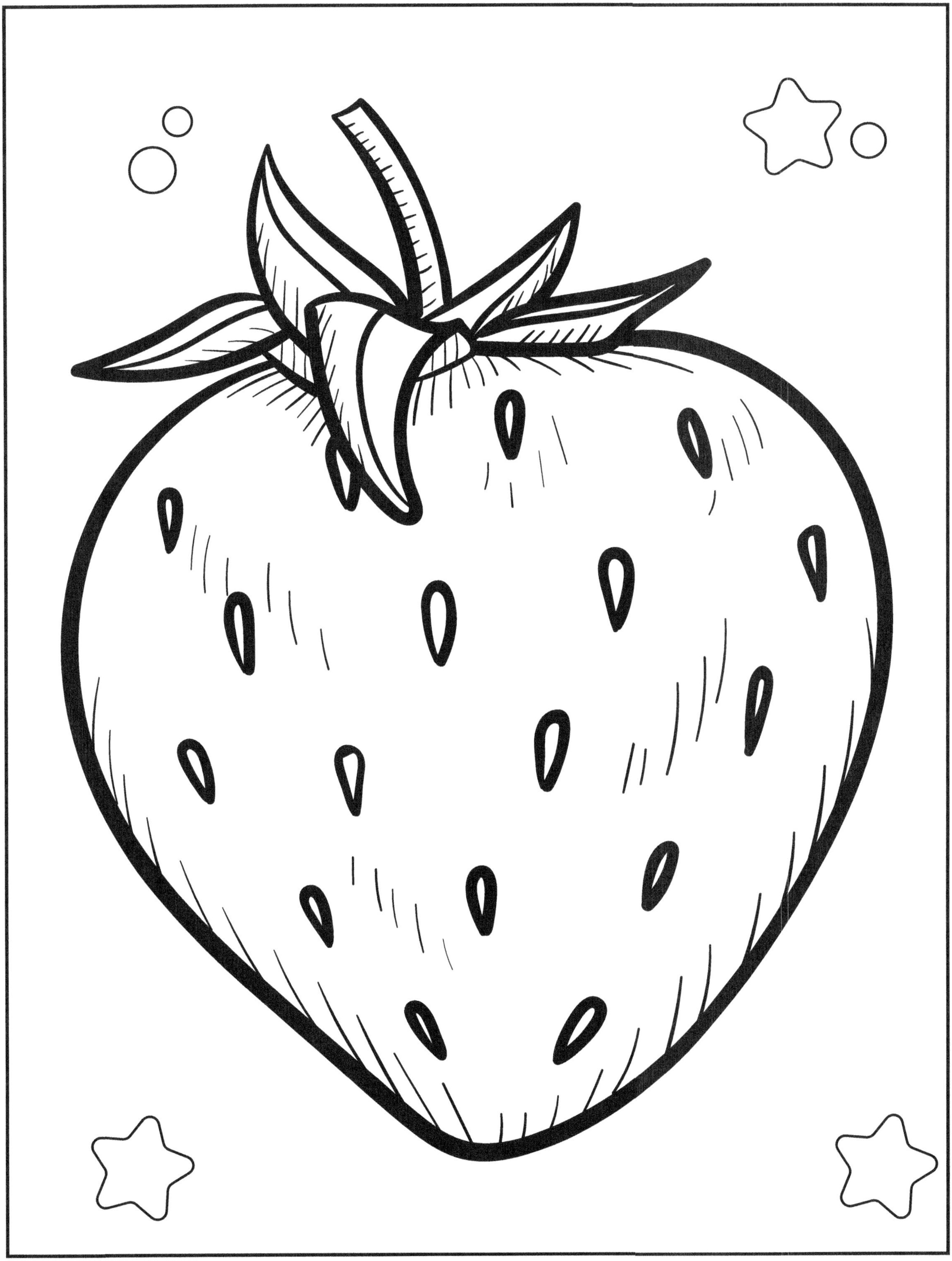

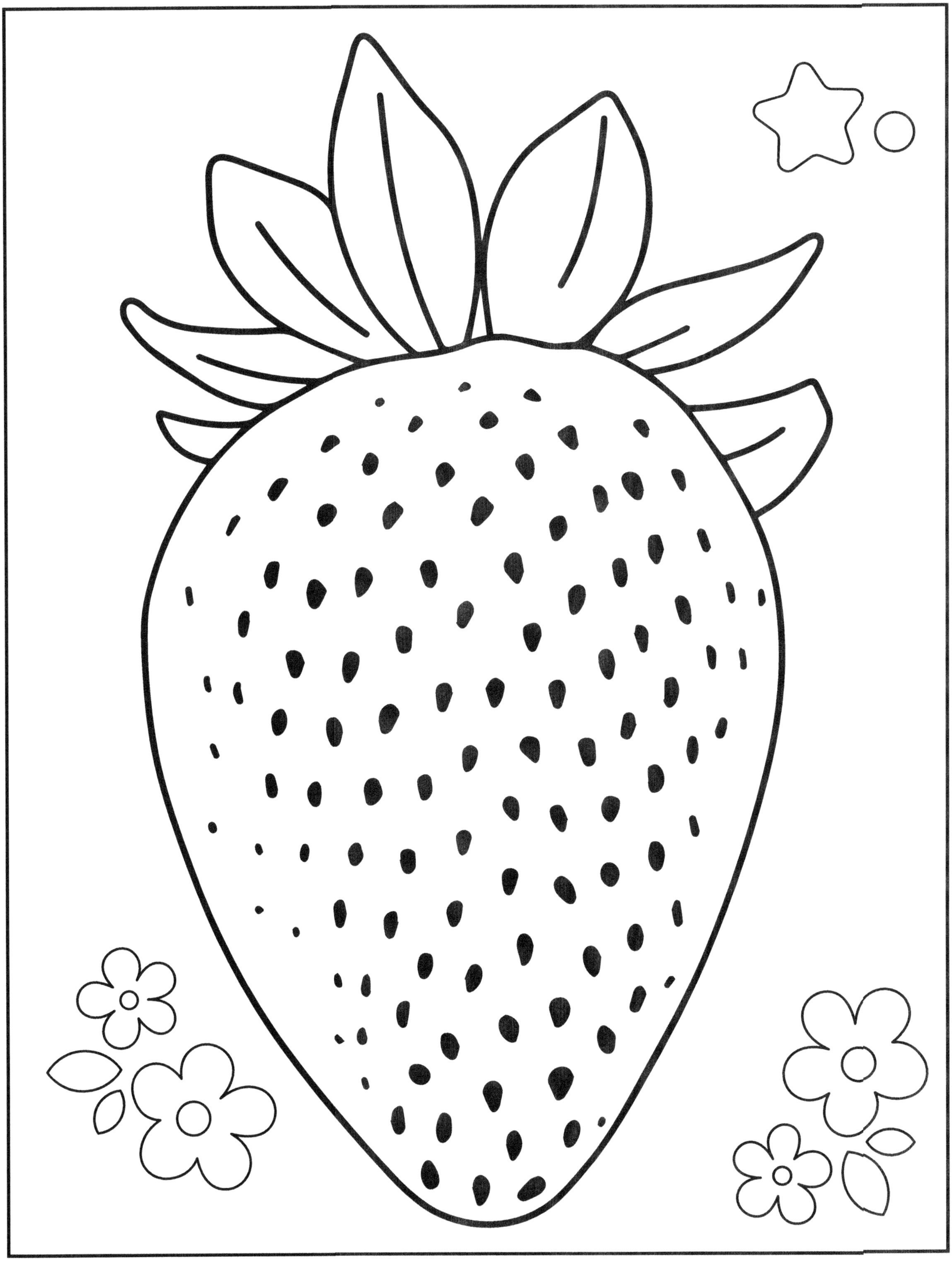

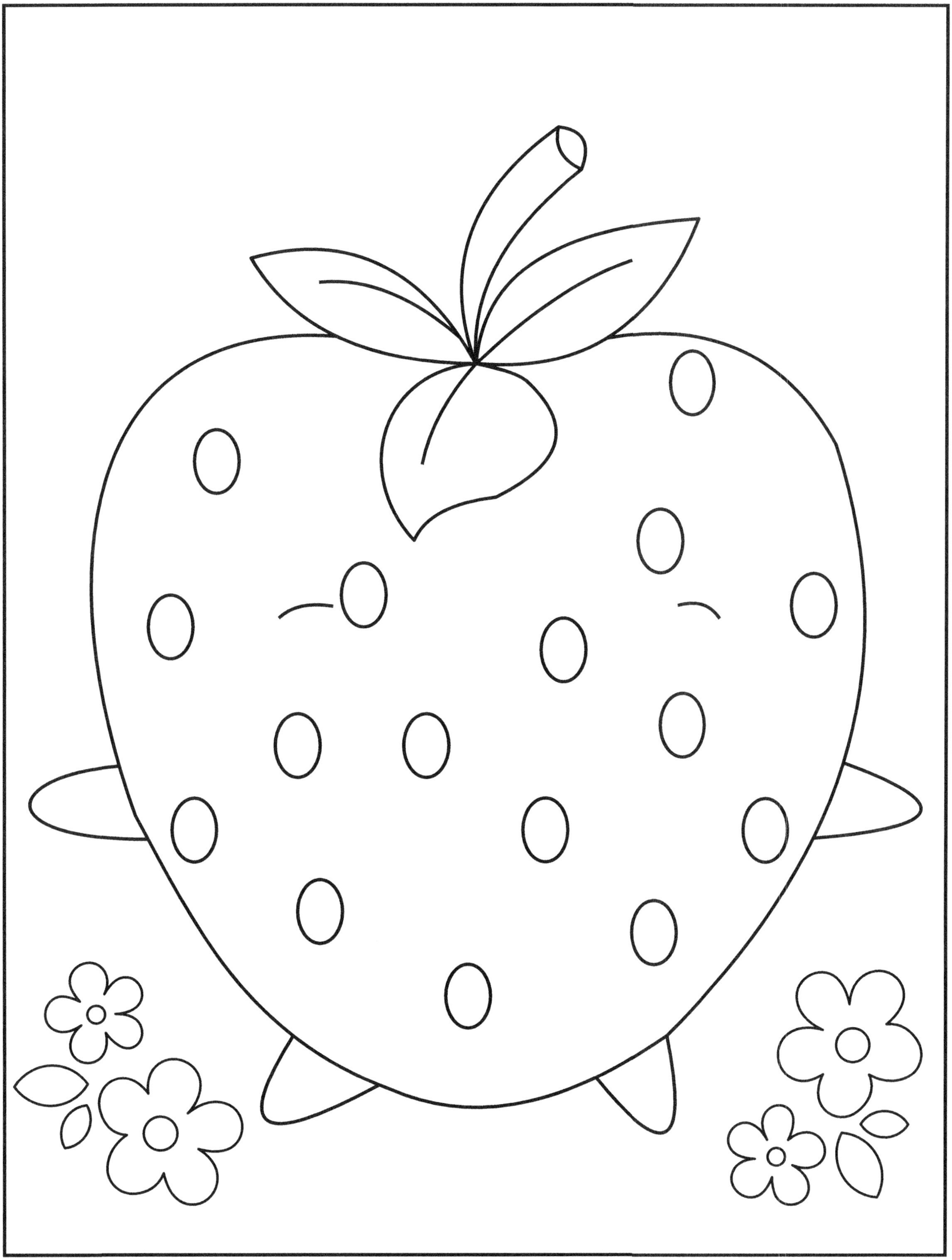

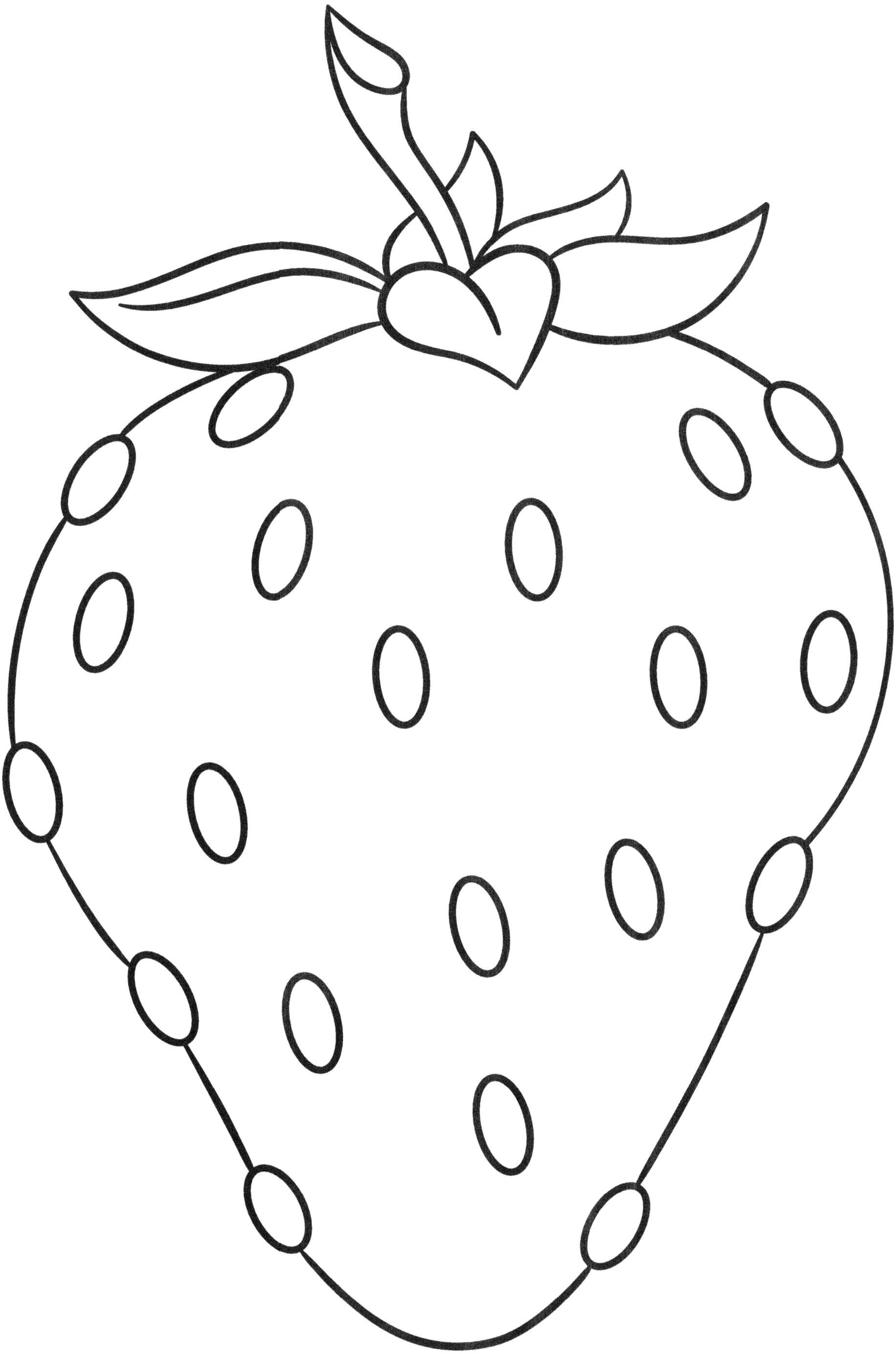

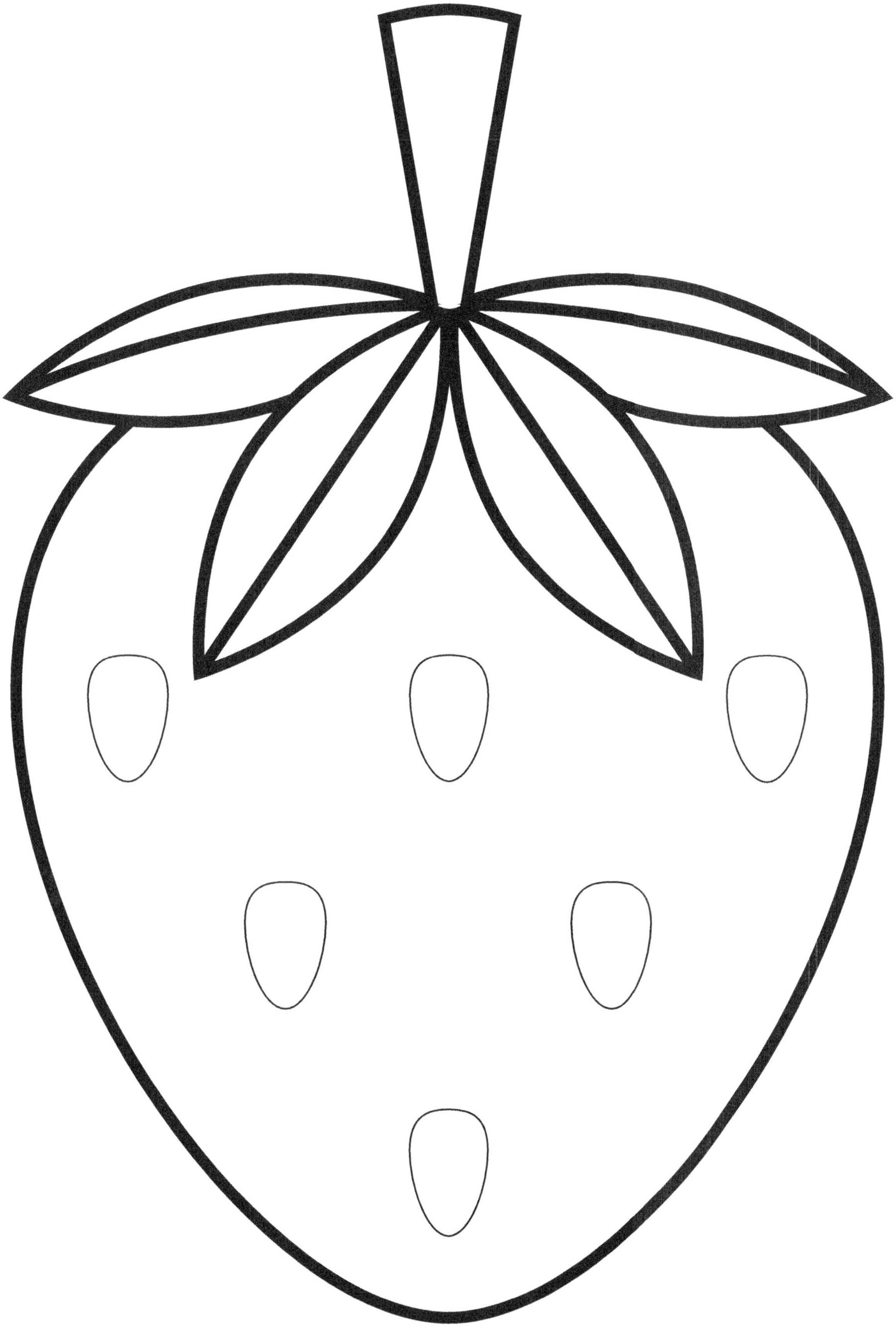

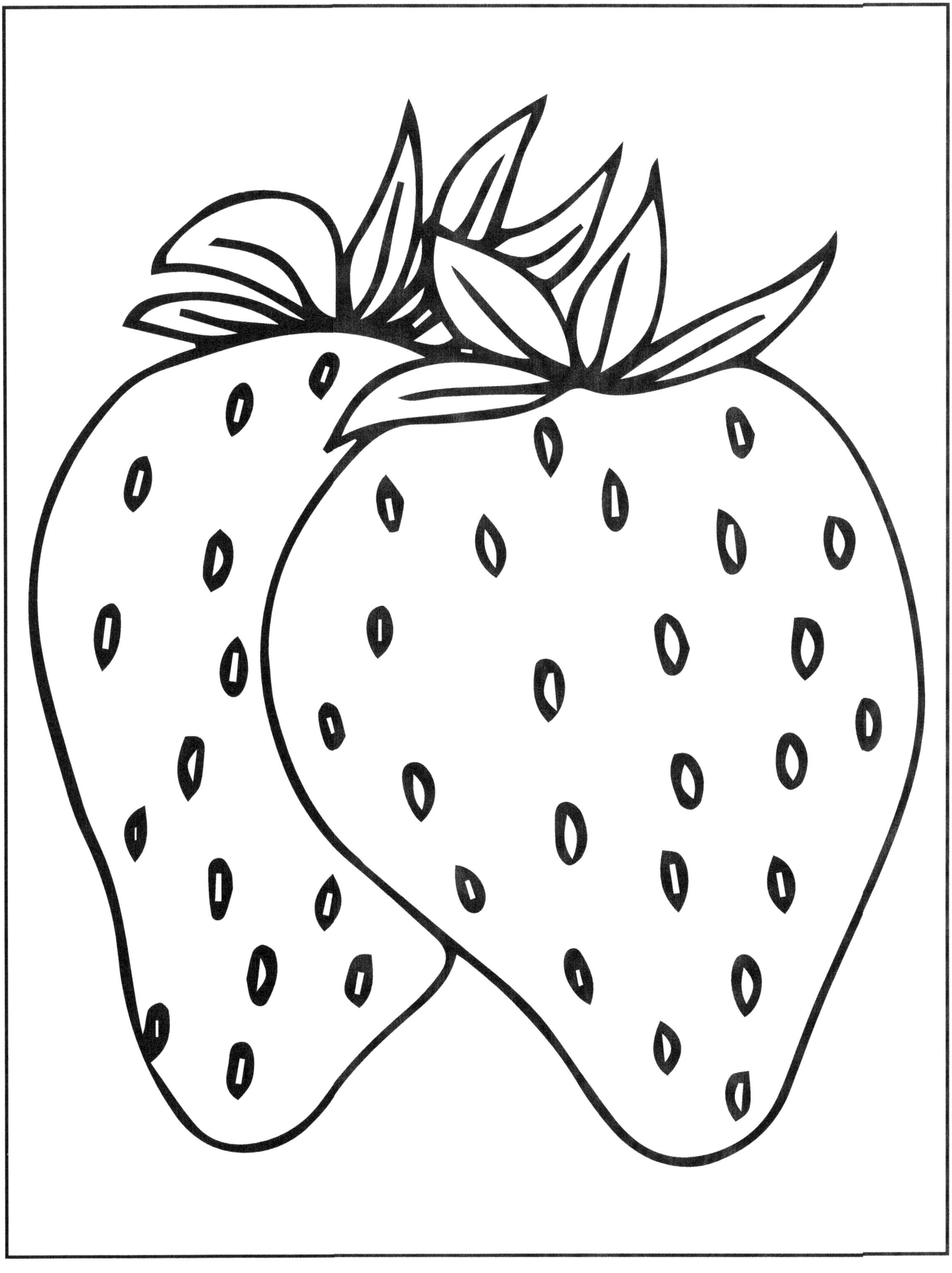

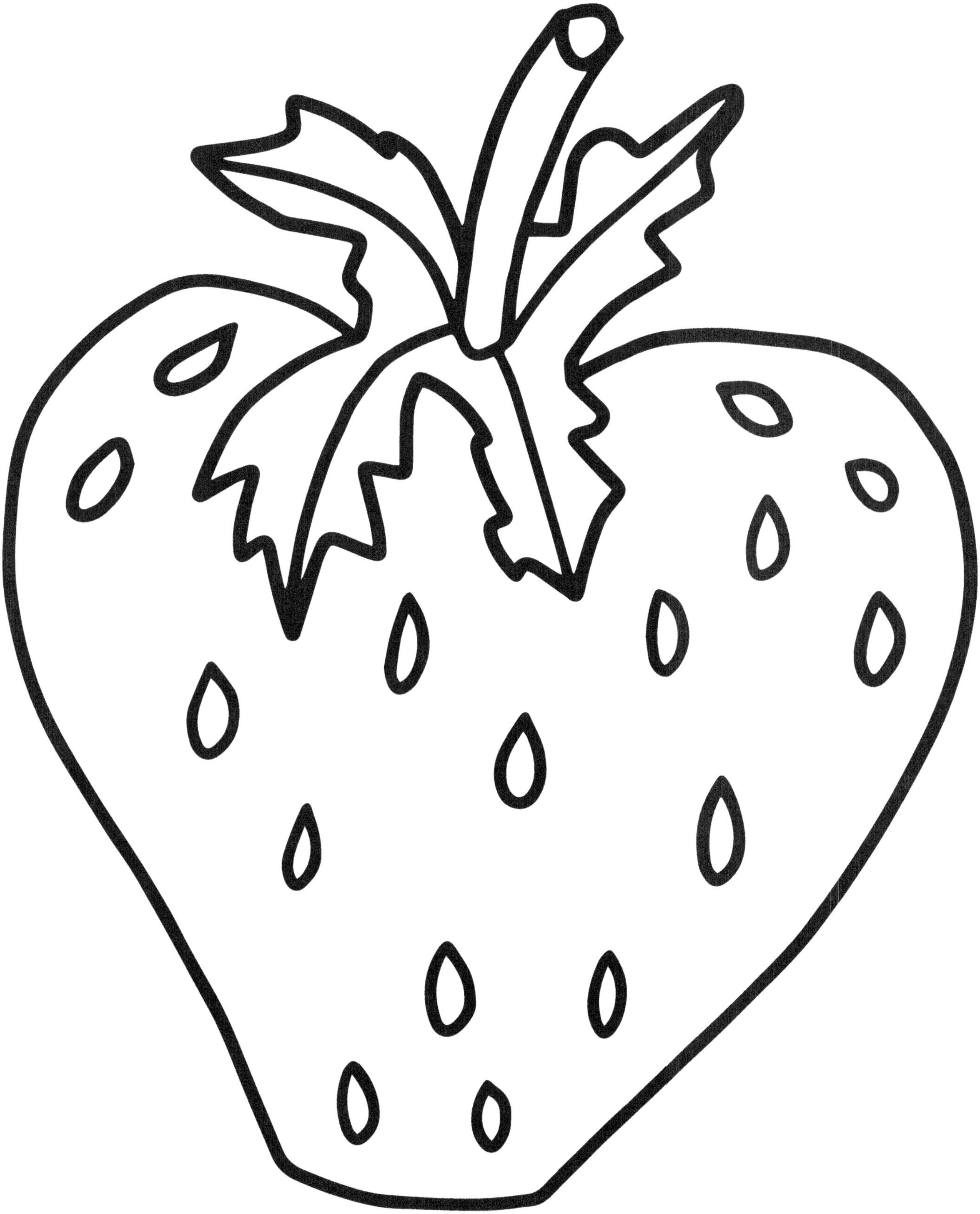

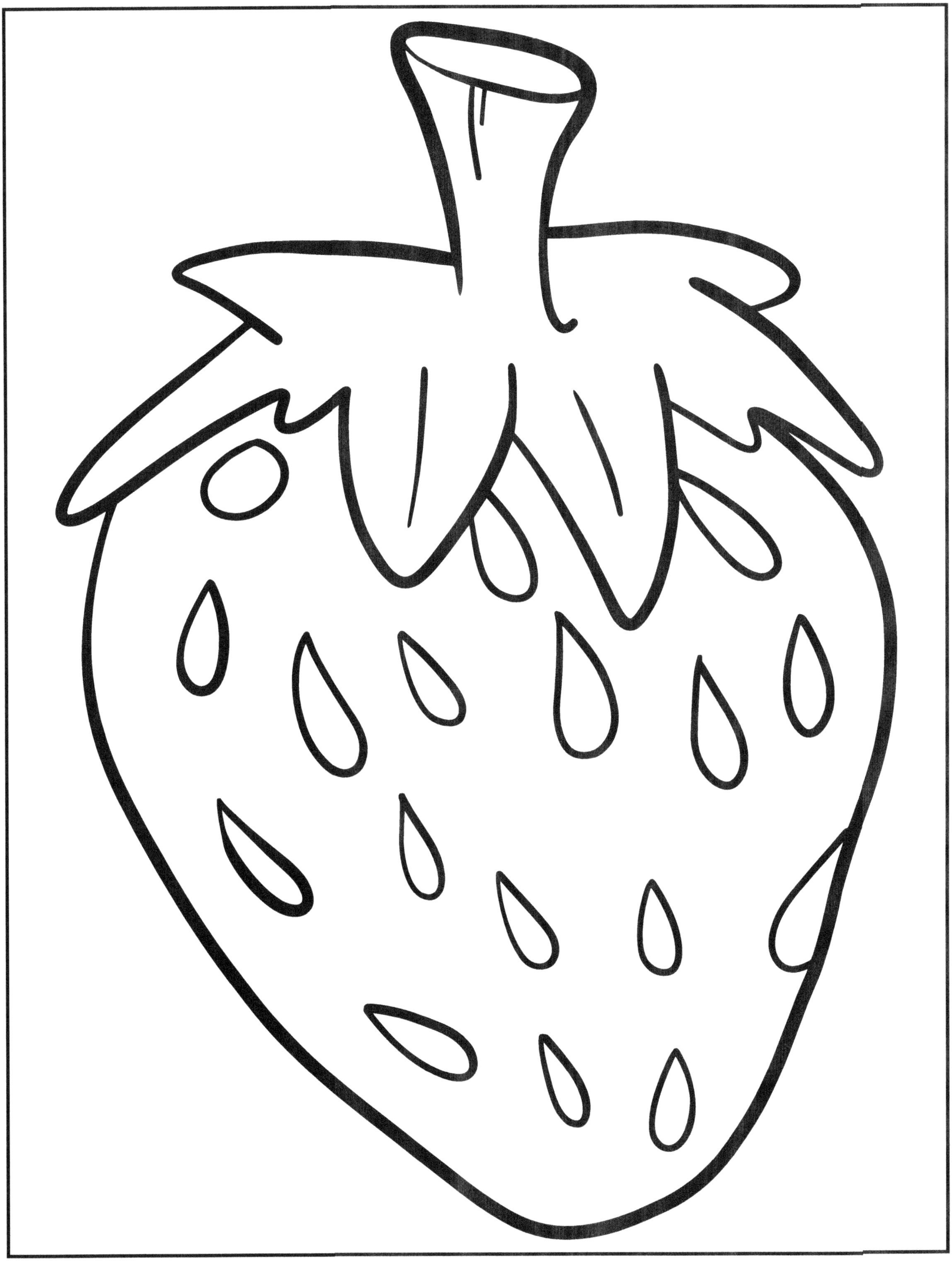

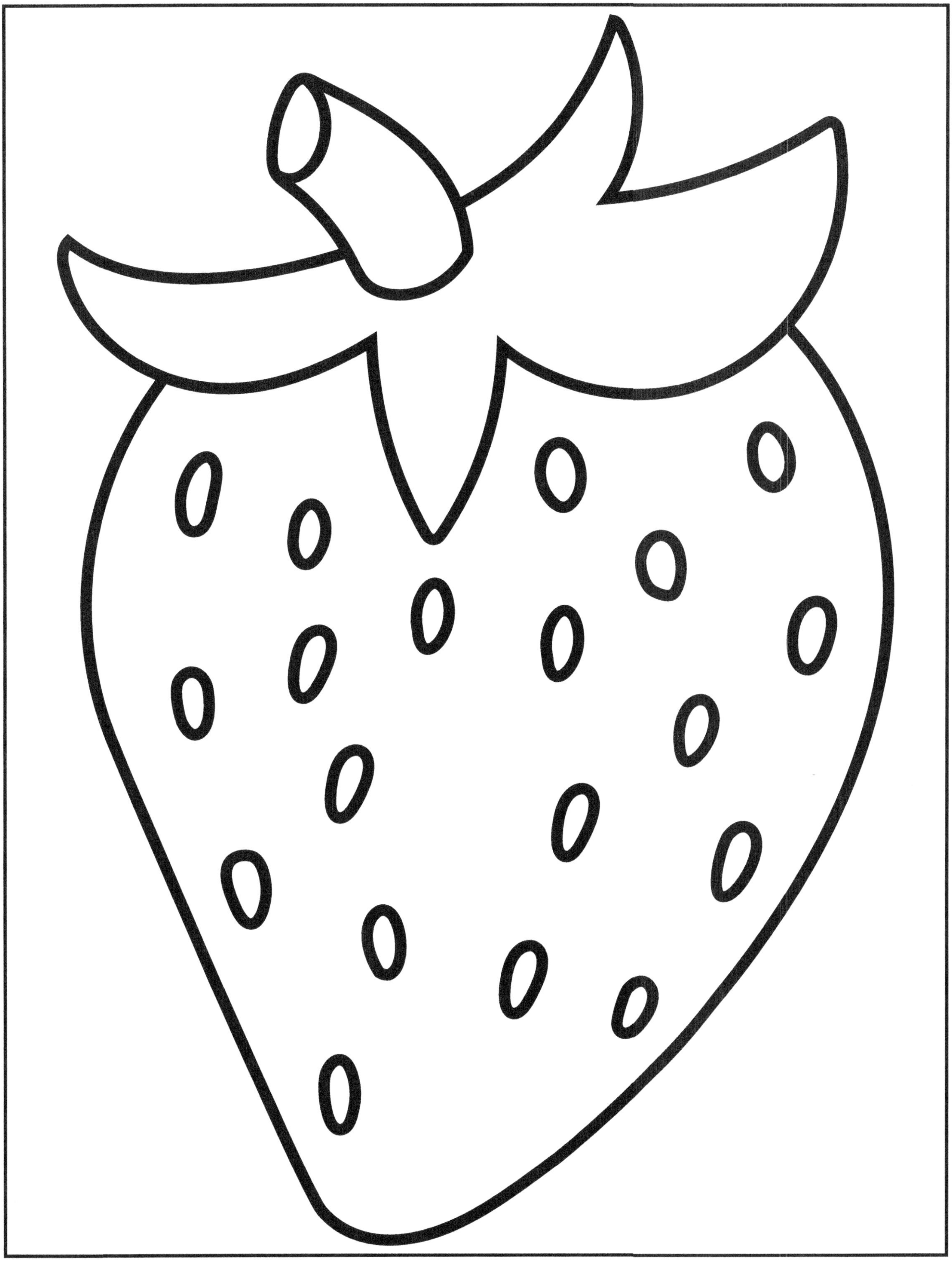

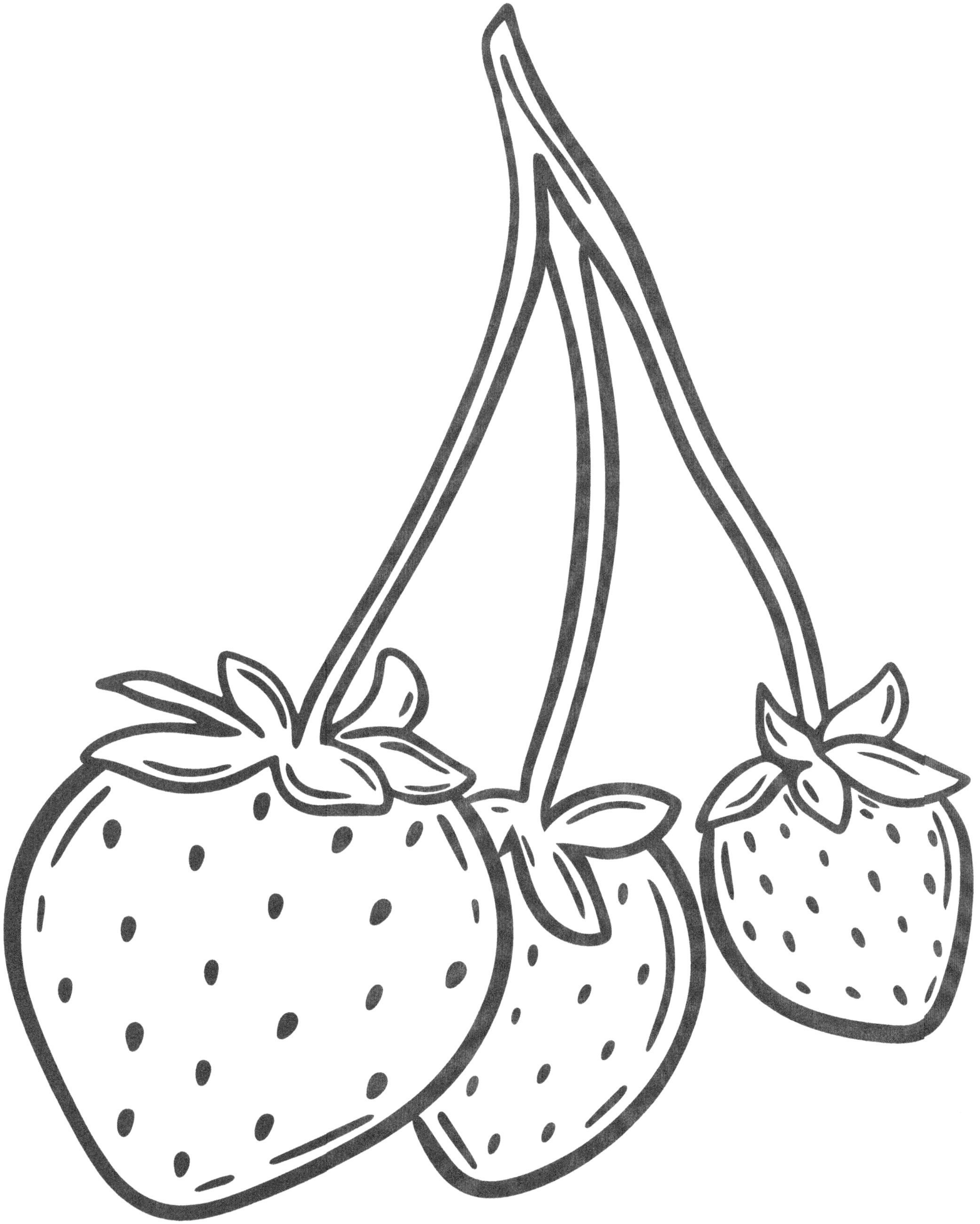

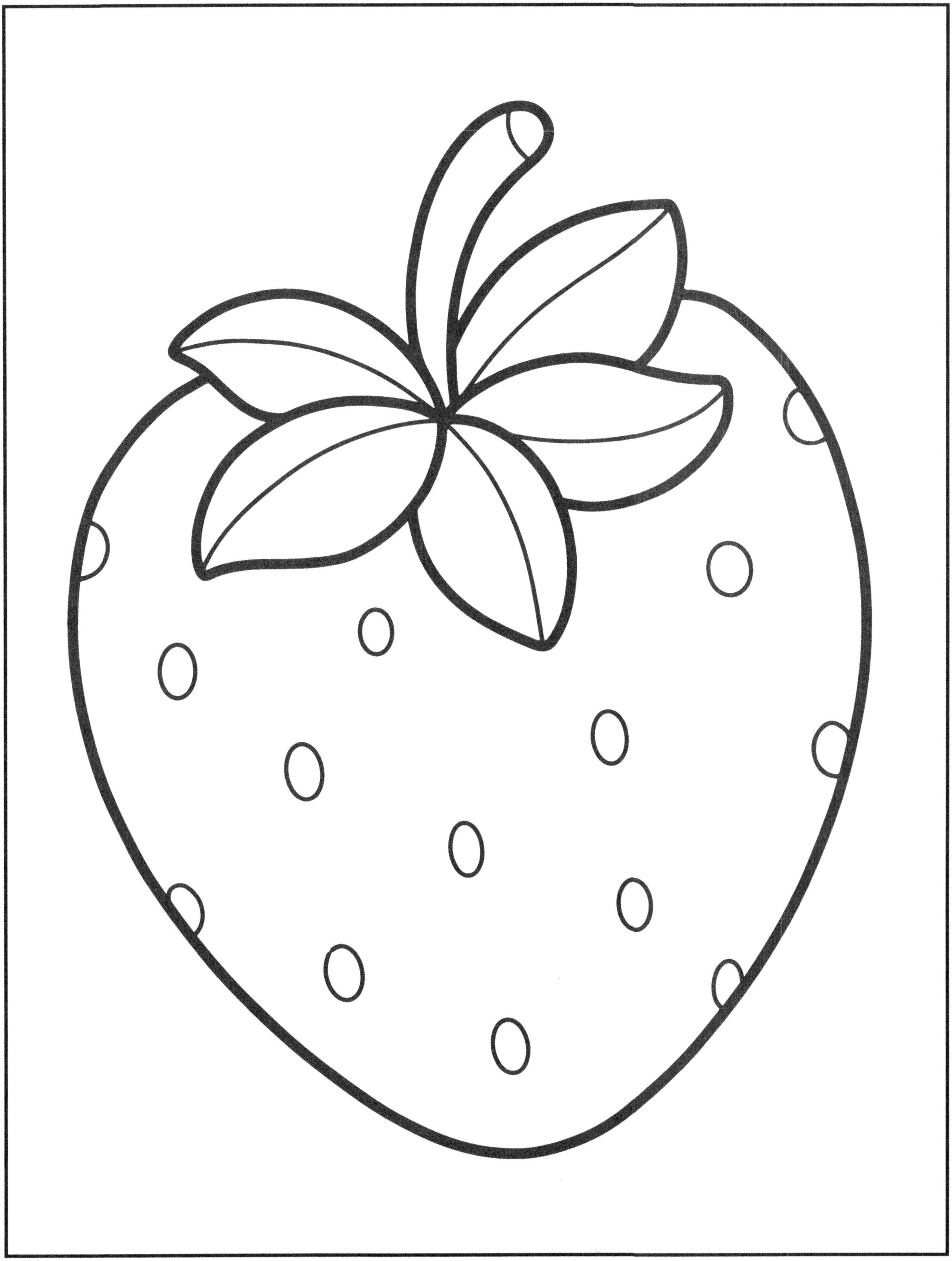

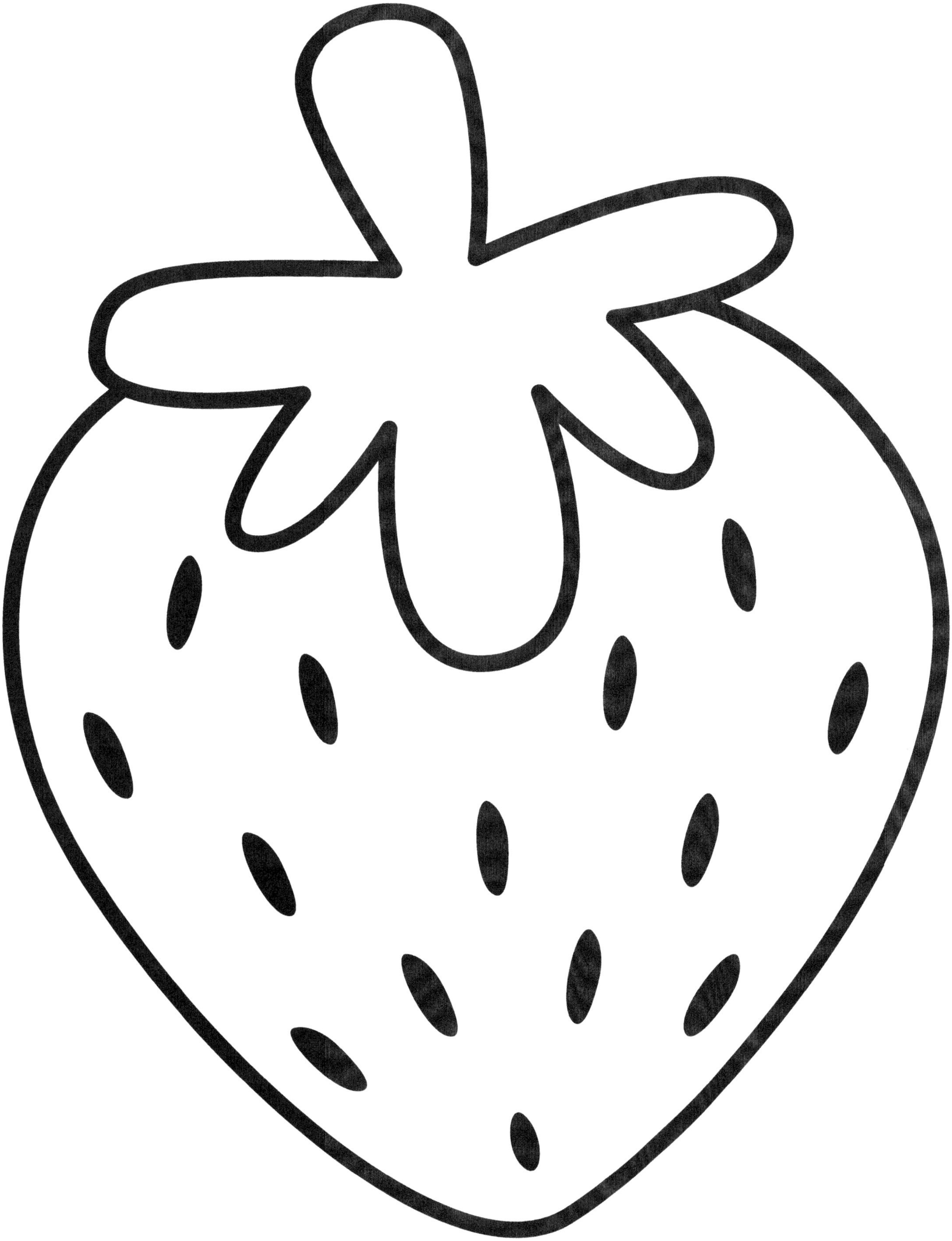

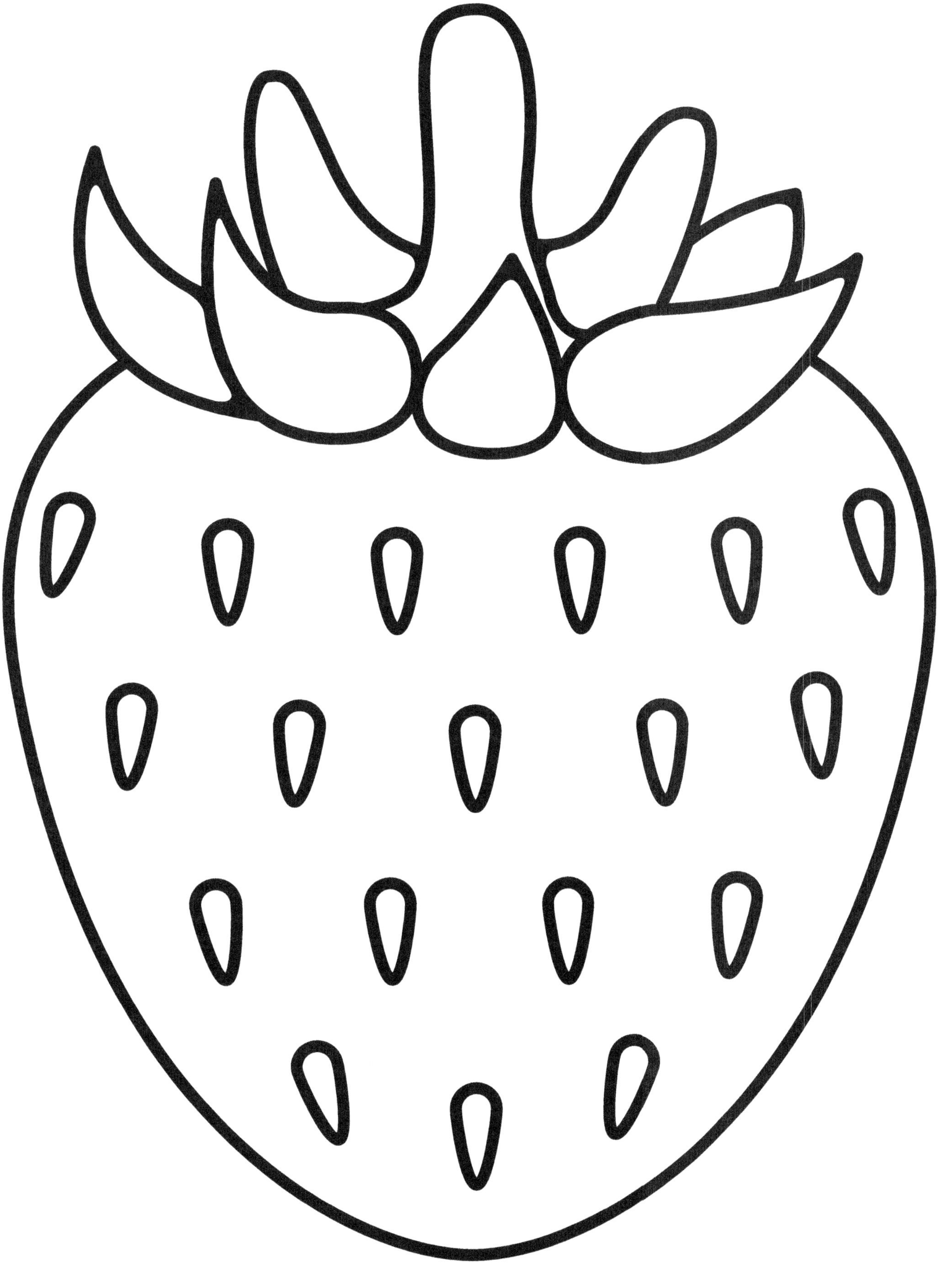

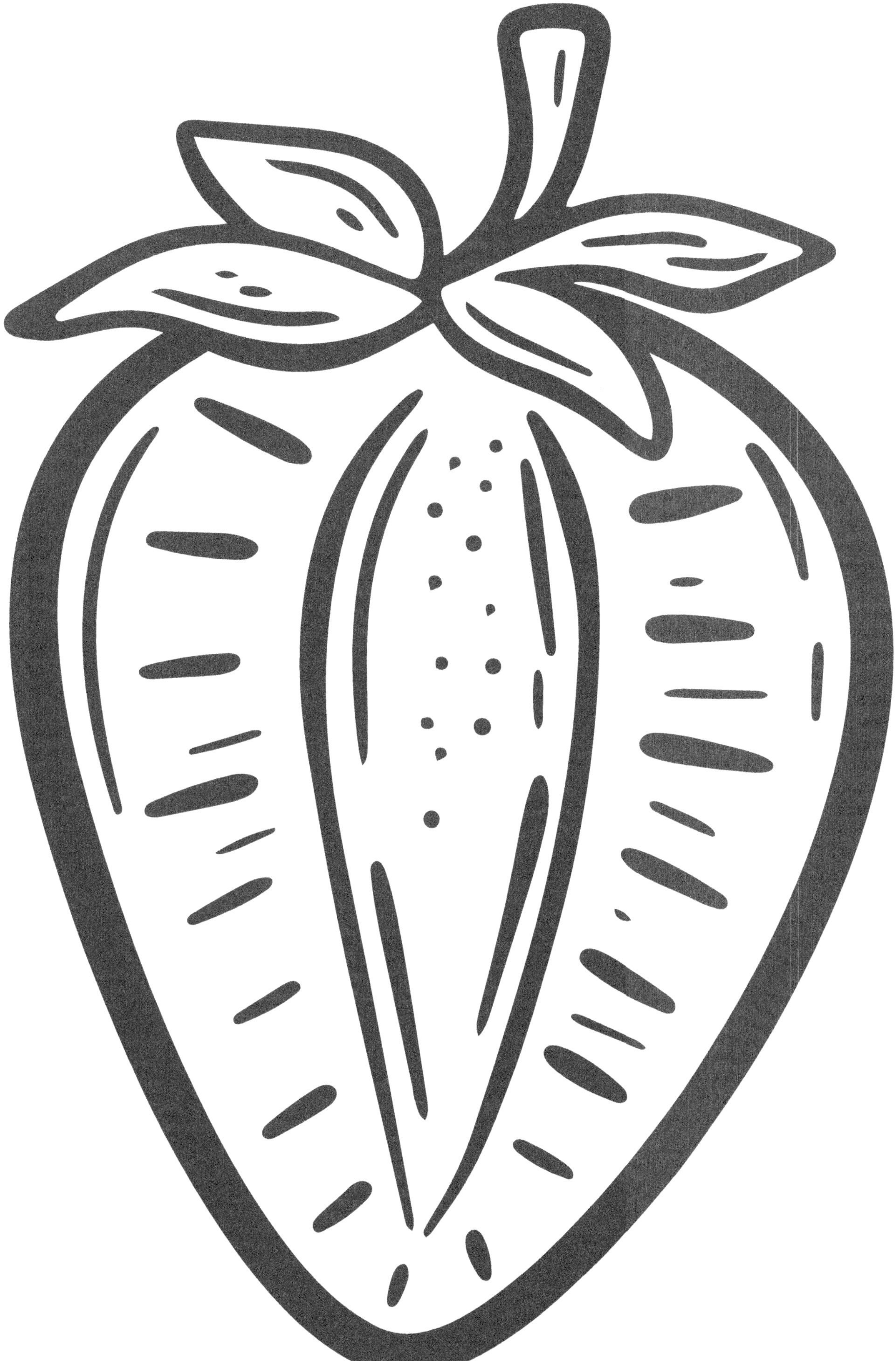

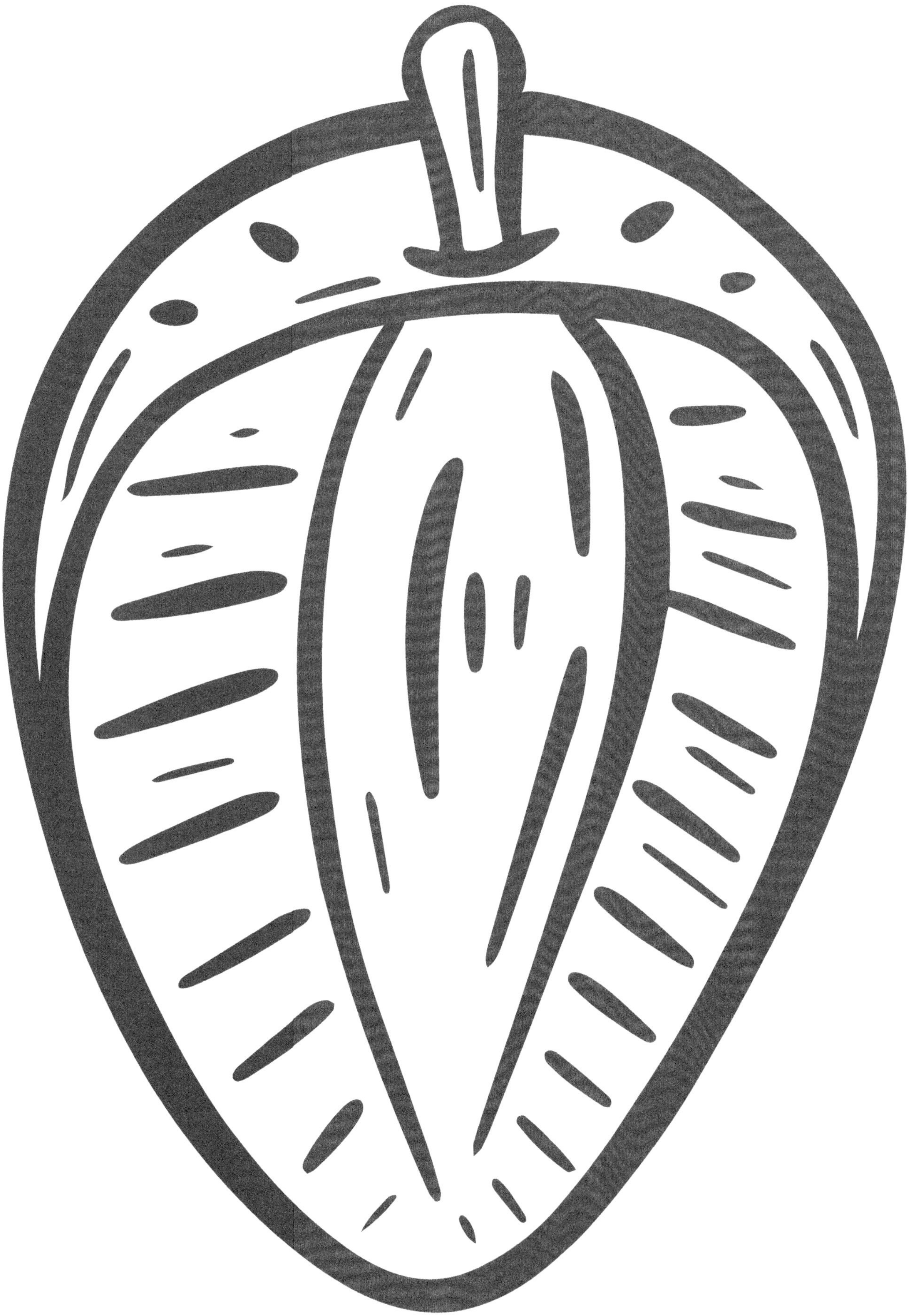

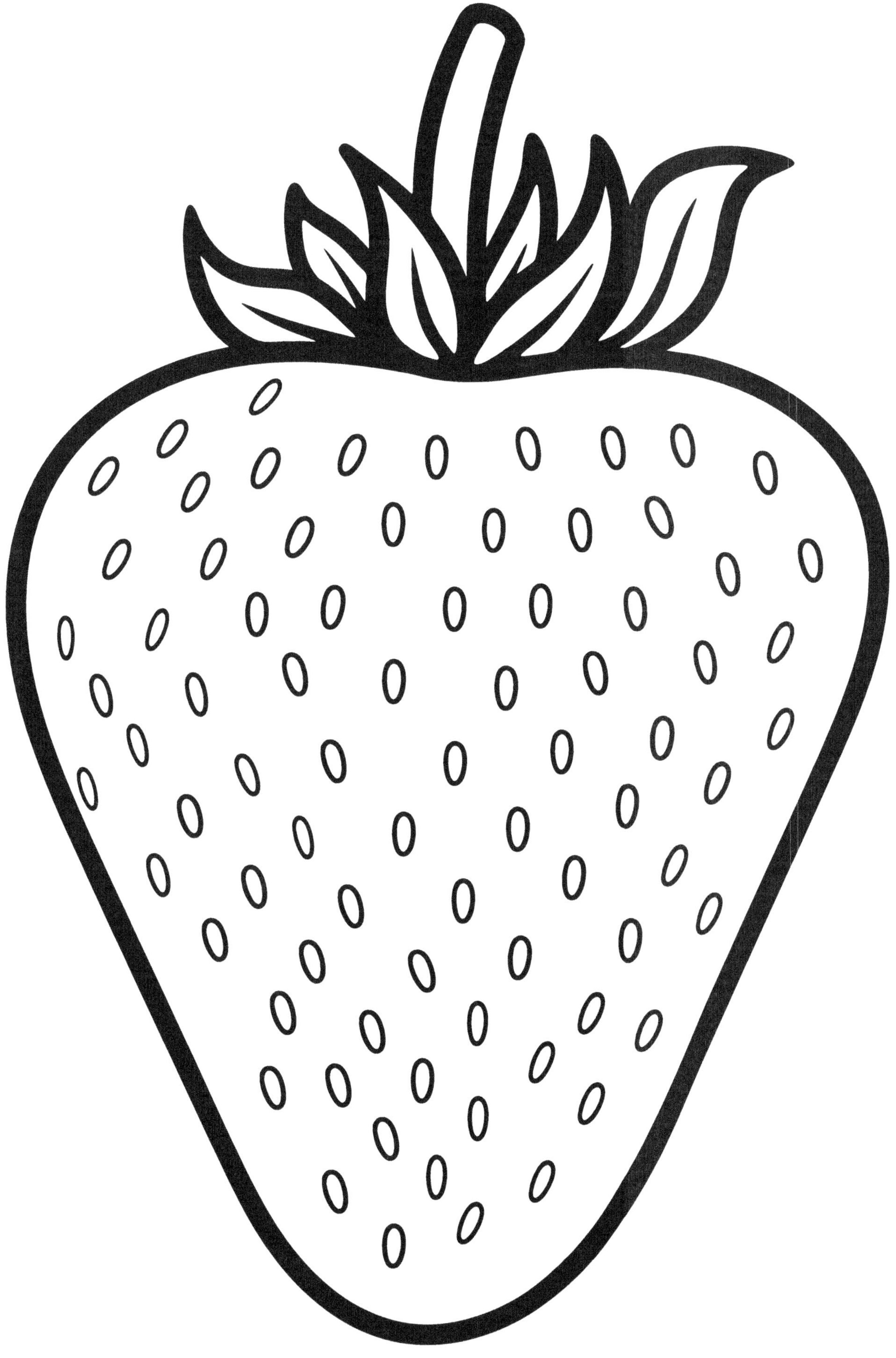

THANKS FOR BEING WITH US I HOPE WE ARE IMPROVED YOUR KIDS EDUCATION

Printed in Great Britain
by Amazon

59180959R00057